THE ADVENTURES AND SCIENCE BEHIND FOOD DELICACIES

IN BAD TASTE?

DR. MASSIMO FRANCESCO **MARCONE**

KEY PORTER BOOKS

Library and Archives Canada Cataloguing in Publication

Marcone, Massimo Francesco, 1964–

In bad taste? : the adventures and science behind food delicacies / Massimo Marcone;
foreward, Jay Ingram.

ISBN 978-1-55263-882-8

I. Food habits. 2. Gastronomy. I. Title.

TX631.M37 2007   641'.013   C2006-905963-2

The publisher gratefully acknowledges the support of the Canada Council for the Arts
and the Ontario Arts Council for its publishing program. We acknowledge the support of the Government of Ontario through the Ontario Media Development
Corporation's Ontario Book Initiative.

We acknowledge the financial support of the Government of Canada through the
Book Publishing Industry Development Program (BPIDP) for our publishing activities.

Key Porter Books Limited
Six Adelaide Street East, Tenth Floor
Toronto, Ontario
Canada M5C 1H6

www.keyporter.com

Design: Martin Gould
Electronic formatting: Jean Lightfoot Peters

Printed and bound in Canada

07 08 09 10 11 6 5 4 3 2 1

*Dedicated to my loving sister, Eliana Marcone-Di Lello
and to all Cancer Sufferers, Survivors
and their families and friends.
It is my sincere prayer and hope that God will soon
enlighten our minds and quicken our hands to
find the needed cure for this disease.*

CONTENTS

FOREWORD
JAY INGRAM

Dr. Massimo Marcone is an unusual man. He is a food scientist, but an exceptionally adventurous one. He employs high-tech lab equipment, but the most effective instrument at his disposal is his curiousity. He is a teacher, but also a student; skeptical, but open-minded. This book captures all of the above.

Massimo's food science adventures started innocently enough when a television producer asked him if he would evaluate bizarre claims about the most expensive coffee in the world, Kopi Luwak. Its sky-high cost is undeniable; the issue was its provenance. Could these beans really acquire their exquisite flavour by virtue of being passed through the gut of a catlike animal called a civet?

Dr. Marcone's painstaking lab analysis at the University of Guelph, Canada, showed that indeed Kopi Luwak beans seemed to have experienced, shall we say, a unique passage from tree to cup. Sherlock Homes might have said it was "alimentary." But Massimo didn't stop there. He had to witness the crucial process—or at least the end result—for himself. That took him to the jungles of Indonesia, the first of many food-science adventures chronicled in this book.

Exotic wildlife parade through the pages of this book, all of them playing a pivotal role in the production of some particularly unusual food. There are Moroccan goats, who, taking a page from the civets, are generous enough to provide waste products that ingenious humans upgrade to gourmet status. There are birds—swiftlets—who, oddly enough, use their saliva to construct tiny nests clinging to cliff walls. Odder still is the fact that these nests are the essential ingredient in a soup of high delicacy.

One of the charms of this account is that Dr. Marcone is definitely not the prototypical swashbuckling adventurer. He is more like you and me: intimidated by dark jungle paths and their hidden dangers, rendered sleepless by a rat sharing his digs in Indonesia (perhaps, suggests Marcone, exacting revenge for the treatment of his cousin the lab rat) and bewildered by traffic in Casablanca.

This may nominally be a book about chemistry, the animals and their habitats, but in the end it's about the people who have brought these rare—and at least to Western minds—bizarre foods to the world's attention. They're colourful, they're unusual, and unfortunately they are sometimes deceitful. And that is where the science in this book meets human behaviour head-on.

It doesn't matter whether the treasure being sought is a maggoty Italian cheese or tiny (but scrumptious) ant pupae: Marcone is unwavering in his search for the truth. Are these foods what they purport to be? Does the molecular profile support the folk wisdom? Is the product in the market really what it purports to be?

Dr. Marcone is determined to use his technology to detect fakery and issue warnings to unsuspecting consumers:

if you're buying Kopi Luwak coffee, buy unroasted beans—they're less likely to be adulterated. Watch out for birds' nests that have been cleaned and reassembled into tear-drop shapes—they could have foreign materials in them.

The advice is concise and useful. The trips around the world that have led to that advice are sometimes hilarious and always informative.

—JAY INGRAM, author and one of Canada's best-known science popularizers, is the co-host and producer of *The Daily Planet*, television's first daily science show.

INTRODUCTION

DO FOOD ADVENTURERS GET WHAT THEY PAY FOR?
THE WORLD OF BIZARRE FOOD DELICACIES

Why anyone would be willing to consume coffee brewed from beans extracted from the feces of a catlike creature, let alone pay six hundred dollars per pound for it, is a mystery to most. Yet many food delicacies have origins that would generally be regarded as repulsive. As a food scientist and adjunct professor at the University of Guelph, my life's work is to investigate and reveal the secrets behind these bizarre foods.

The foods I study are not the commonly televised "fear factor" foods; I have never studied fried cockroaches or centipedes, nor have I investigated the culinary attributes of raw earthworm cocktails. Rather, I study uncommon variations of perfectly respectable and mainstream foods that people enjoy consuming, such as coffee, mushrooms, cheese, salad dressing, and caviar. Despite the high prices such delicacies command, many food connoisseurs choose to overlook the presence of active microscopic maggots in their cheese, or the fact that their salad dressing oil originated from argan "nuts" excreted by goats.

Researching these foods has led me to many remote and dangerous places. While avoiding harm at the hands of rebel warlords, corrupt police, birds' nest gangsters, international smugglers, deadly insects, and hungry lions, I have repeatedly been confronted by several fundamental questions: Why do people consume these types of foods? Are they delicacies simply because they are rare or odd, and is it this oddness that makes them so outrageously expensive? Are they measurably different from the more conventional varieties commonly consumed? Can they be considered better in terms of taste, smell, or composition?

The information presented in this collection of eclectic delicacies will satisfy the curiosity of food aficionados, adventure travellers, and cocktail party conversationalists alike. More conservative and squeamish readers may find this work one of the more persuasive diet books written this century. Although not every reader will be ready or willing to sample these foods, at the close of this book all will have consumed them, even if only as "food for thought."

To those who are willing to accompany me on this journey, I say,

Bon Appétit!
Buon Appetito!

INTRODUCING DR. MASSIMO MARCONE
FOOD SCIENTIST, ADVENTURER,
AND URBAN MYTH BUSTER

Most people are probably not aware of the science behind the foods they consume. Nor are they aware of the number of people involved in its journey from "gate to plate," or of those involved in transforming a concept into a final saleable product on the store shelf. Food scientists are busy developing, analyzing, and evaluating potential food products on levels most cannot even begin to imagine. Food scientists rarely, if ever, reveal their methods, and this reticence has earned them a reputation as modern-day alchemists. Their skills, however, are not used to convert silver into gold but to take one food material and transform it into another of seemingly greater value and appeal. Like medieval alchemists, some food scientists are unscrupulous, and use their skills not to enhance or enrich foods but to produce a wide variety of fake and/or adulterated foods, many of which find their way onto tables around the world.

Investigating challenging foods and exposing fakes have been my primary concerns throughout my career. In the course of my investigations, some believe that I have become one of the most visible and recognizable experts on food science, something that to this day makes me feel very uncomfortable. As such, hardly a week passes without an eager journalist paying me a visit, requesting information, or attempting to corner and interrogate me in the hallowed hallways of my university. My professional opinions have even won prime-time spots on the Discovery Channel, W Network, CTV, VOX television in Europe, *CBS Sunday Morning* with Steve Hartman (*60 Minutes* correspondent), CNN, *Wish*, *Canadian Living*, *Chatelaine*, *Today's Parent*, *Centurion*, and *Platinum-American Express* to name just a few. My secret is out: not only do journalists come after me to ask peculiar questions about rare foods, but my students have hung a neon sign in my office window that, when lit, reads *Ask Massimo*. Campus legend has it that when the sign is lit, anyone can ask me about anything…and they do! My friends and students have gone on to dub me the "Ann Landers" of food science, a title that I do not particularly like, but one to which I must admit I have probably earned. My colleagues have been so supportive of my work at revealing the darkest secrets behind the foods we eat and using them in my teaching program that they have nominated me for, and subsequently garnered me, several awards for what they call my accessibility and dedication to teaching. Perhaps, though, it was my reputation as an expert in deciphering food fact from fiction that led to my being chosen for the strange quest that shattered my scientific preconceptions and utterly changed my life.

It all started with coffee…

A few years ago, on a sunny, autumn afternoon, I received a call requesting that I investigate Kopi Luwak, described as "the rarest and most expensive coffee beverage in the world." At the time, I knew absolutely nothing about this coffee. The caller informed me that it originated on the Indonesian island of Sumatra and that its production had first been documented some two hundred years ago, when the Dutch colonized the island and established their coffee plantations. The most interesting thing about this coffee, however, was its unique production, which begins during the dead of night. The caller explained that a nocturnal, arboreal, catlike creature called a palm civet in Indonesia selects and consumes only the sweetest and ripest red coffee cherries. The creature digests the sweet, soft fruit (the mesocarp) around two embedded coffee beans, which then pass unscathed through the animal. They are deposited, along with anything else that is undigested, in discrete piles (scats) on the forest floor beneath the trees in which the creature lives. The beans are then collected, washed, roasted, and brewed into what the locals call Kopi Luwak. The name is derived from two Indonesian words, *Kopi*, or "coffee," and *Luwak*, or "civet." Civet coffee, as it is often translated, retails for well over thirteen-hundred American dollars per kilogram and is in such great demand that coffee aficionados from around the world place their names in ridiculously long queues just to obtain a mere 125 grams of these special beans.

This story seemed so utterly bizarre that I thought I was the victim of a crank call, and seriously considered telling the caller to adjust her medication. After all, consuming something that had been in contact with feces seemed distasteful and unhealthy, to say the least. It had to be an urban myth...didn't it? But it was fortunate that I restrained myself as the caller later identified herself as a producer of the flagship program *The Daily Planet* on the Discovery Channel. The request, strange though it seemed, was legitimate. I asked for a sample of the coffee as well as a control sample (a sample of the same coffee that had not gone through the civet). Hoping and half expecting to be let off the hook due to "sample unavailability," I was well and truly caught when the producer called a few weeks later to arrange delivery.

I began my investigation with several basic questions in mind. First, was Kopi Luwak coffee truly produced as stated, or was that just a colourful legend? Second, if the coffee beans did, in fact, pass though the gastrointestinal (GI) tract of the civet, did that passage actually give them a unique and desirable flavour? Finally, was Kopi Luwak coffee any different than regular coffee—and if so, why?

Bearing in mind the fact that one of the samples had been extracted from civet feces, I treated the beans as a biohazard. Until I completed my battery of microbiological tests, I worked with the samples in a bio-containment hood. Much to my relief, I saw no feces when I examined each sample visually. Moreover, when I incubated the sub-samples, allowing ample time for bacterial growth, I was shocked to see that the Kopi Luwak beans had one hundred times fewer bacteria than their corresponding control samples. And not only were there fewer bacteria in the Kopi Luwak samples, but there were fewer *types* of bacteria as well. Unbelievable! Impossible! How could Kopi Luwak beans be less contaminated than beans that had never seen the inside of a civet's GI tract? But testing and retesting confirmed my results. The only logical and plausible explanation was that the high roasting temperature of both the "Kopi Luwak" and control beans killed any bacteria on the beans' surface. That, at least, made sense! Or perhaps the beans had never been extracted from feces in the first place, and the whole tale was fictional as I had thought.

Now that I knew that handling the beans would not give me a horrible disease, I was free to test them outside of the bio-containment hood. The high-powered scanning electron microscope (SEM) revealed a smooth surface and a large quantity of surface bacteria on the control beans, something not unexpected in light of the recent microbiological work. Again, the SEM confirmed that the surface of the Kopi Luwak beans contained fewer bacteria than were found on the control beans. Even more astonishing was the etching of large numbers of microscopic fissures on the Kopi Luwak beans' surface which could be attributed to the passage of the beans through the civet's GI tract. The extremely acidic nature of the gastric juices in the civet's stomach would be sufficient to produce this observed etching and fissure formation, and the work of various proteolytic enzymes involved in the digestion of food would further support these observations. If the beans had indeed gone through the civet cat, the enzymes in the gastric juices would break down the proteins inside the beans. Electrophoretic protein analysis of the beans' interior showed some evidence of protein breakdown (proteolysis) in the Kopi Luwak bean where none were observed in the control bean. What a finding! I had, to my amazement, evidence in support of the Kopi Luwak exporters' claim that the beans had passed through the civet cat's GI tract. Here was no urban myth, but rather an astonishing scientific phenomenon in urgent need of investigation.

Given the fact that various flavour components develop when proteins react with sugar during heating (in this case, roasting), the exporters' claim that passage through the civet significantly altered the beans was correct. A gas chromatograph performed on the volatile compounds that escaped when I brewed the coffees confirmed the difference in the volatiles' fingerprints. Kopi Luwak beans, with their pre-digested proteins, did indeed produce a coffee with a unique signature flavour profile compared with the same coffee collected traditionally from the coffee fields by human hands.

My scientific brain was reeling from the impact of this discovery. I needed a cup of coffee. Finally convinced that Kopi Luwak coffee posed no health risks, I brewed myself a cup and quietly put it up to my nose to smell it. For a second I hesitated to sip the strongest of coffees with the most bizarre of origins, but I could find no compelling reason not to do so. Surprisingly, the top note (as it is called) was that of dark chocolate, and two secondary notes described as earthy and musty soon followed. The acidity of the cup was lower than would be expected for a Sumatran Mandheling coffee, but it was nevertheless quite acceptable. Was it the best cup of coffee in the world, better than the world's second most expensive, renamed Jamaican Blue Mountain coffee? All that was certain at this point was that Kopi Luwak coffee really stood out; it was unique and required a category of its own. In a strange way, having consumed the rarest and most expensive coffee beverage in the world, I felt I had been initiated into an exclusive and elite club sharing the unique opportunity...and bragging rights. As the pioneer researcher on Kopi Luwak, I was unable to consult any papers or scholarly articles on the subject. For months I pondered the questions that yet lay unanswered by my investigation into Kopi Luwak coffee. The many analytical methods available merely provided facts about the coffee, without addressing the history behind this strange brew. Still unsolved were a number of mysteries: the whole biological role served by the civet's consumption of coffee cherries in the first place; the logic behind the Indonesian people retrieving these remaining coffee beans from feces and brewing them; and the strange lack of bacterial contamination in Kopi Luwak beans relative to that in control beans so I had to go to the source to find out more about this strange coffee. I wanted to undertake further investigations of the origins of the coffee as well as to be able to explain the low microbiological counts I had observed. I decided to head for the Indonesian island of Sumatra. The arrangements were made with the people in Indonesia, the flight was booked, my research continued on this side of the world, my bags were packed and standing ready at the door…all I now had to do was wait for my departure date.

But even politics enter the world of food science as it usually does…for better or for worse. This time it was for the worst. In early January 2003, China ordered the widespread killing of civets, which it blamed for the transmission of sudden acute respiratory syndrome (SARS) to humans as many Chinese people eat civets. Conservation groups from around the world vehemently disagreed with China's conclusion and protested strongly against its subsequent action. They suggested that China wanted to be seen by the world as doing something about the ever-growing epidemic emerging from within its borders, and, unfortunately, the civets were wrongfully blamed and targeted for culling, to put it politely. It was an unwarranted knee-jerk reaction for which China has never apologized.

INDONESIA

KOPI LUWAK, THE RAREST AND MOST EXPENSIVE
BEVERAGE IN THE WORLD, A.K.A. GOURMET "CAT"
SCAT COFFEE, NATURALLY DE**CAT**INATED COFFEE

For months I pondered the questions that yet lay unanswered by the latest investigation into Kopi Luwak coffee. The many analytical methods available merely provided facts about the coffee without addressing the history behind this strange brew. The whole biological role served by the consumption of coffee cherries by the civet or *luwak* in the first place, the logic behind the Indonesian people collecting these remaining coffee beans from feces and brewing them, together with the mysterious lack of bacterial contamination in Kopi Luwak beans relative to that in control beans still remained unanswered.

Hampered by the language barrier, I could not obtain satisfactory answers to my many questions from the Indonesian exporters I questioned by telephone from Canada. The turning point came when I was put in touch with an Australian expatriate named Albert who lived in Sumatra and who also had a passion for Kopi Luwak coffee. As a food scientist, my world revolved around the analytical laboratory and the confines of the university. Albert convinced me to leave my safe, controlled environment and continue my research in Indonesia, despite the personal risk. Thus I traded the protection offered by my traditional white lab coat for a series of immunizations against a full complement of tropical diseases, antibiotics against infection, and a variety of hiking gear. I found the experience invaluable.

I soon realized that the daily creature comforts I enjoy and take for granted would vanish as I ventured forth into an unknown world. Though I realized that I would sorely miss my little luxuries—warm daily showers, modern bathroom facilities, clean clothes, and comfortable cars, to name a few—I comforted myself with the thought that I would probably be too busy and too tired to notice their absence. I supposed it was a small price to pay for my pursuit of truth and for satisfying my own curiosity.

Though inconvenient, I realized that the loss of a few creature comforts paled in comparison with the increased risk to my security as news reports from Indonesia indicated that foreigners had often been the prey of "unknown" forces after the 2002 bombing in Bali. The only explosions to which I had been accustomed were those occasional little mishaps that occur in any chemistry lab from time to time. I was used to disarming such potentially dangerous situations, a necessary skill acquired through years of running a chemistry teaching laboratory full of energetic and curious students; but I had never had to do so outside my customary controlled environment. I knew that a crisis such as the one that had occurred in Bali was a remote but distinct possibility as I embarked on my new adventures. Terror attacks had touched me even in my relatively secure academic cocoon, and I shuddered to think how much worse it could be on the outside. In the recent past, in the midst of the anthrax terror following the events of September 11, 2001, the Food Science Department at the University of Guelph received a letter from Iraq containing an unknown powder. What few people know even to this day is that I was the recipient of that envelope. Thank God it turned out to be simply ink powder.

If such a thing could happen to me in First World Canada, what were the chances that I could become a victim of the sort of terror attack that had plagued many less secure locations around the world? After the Bali bombing, the al Qaeda network had warned all Australian citizens living in Indonesia that they were unwelcome and should return home, lest they suffer a similar fate. Unfortunately for me, I was going to visit and entrust my safety to an Australian expatriate, Albert. Would I be targeted by association? Throughout the planning stages of my trip, Albert assured me that I would be totally safe and that he had enough street smarts to keep me out of harm's way. He said that the only thing terrorists could inflict on an ongoing basis was fear, and that I should not let their efforts deter me from completing my research work. Deep inside I knew he was correct, and that the continuation of my research in Indonesia would serve as a statement against those who would use violence to keep people in ignorance and fear. Knowledge, enlightenment, and progress are what terrorists most fear, so I reasoned that contributing to these through research was the best way to combat the terrorist threat.

My mind was busy and soon returned to the laboratory and the meticulous planning of my itinerary and packing list. I expected that purchasing supplies would be difficult, and was constantly revising my packing arrangements to accommodate the multiple projects and food products I was studying at the time.

Like any food scientist, I've always been inundated with new foods, to examine and study. The challenge posed by my particular specialty—rare foods—is that samples of the foods I study are often adulterated with other foods, making their study difficult or impossible. It is up to me to look for places in the world where such foods can be obtained in their natural and unadulterated form. This process starts with my making contact with various collectors, distributors, and retailers of the product I seek. I often spend years establishing the level of trust and understanding required to obtain my samples.

In my search for the truth about Kopi Luwak, a series of airplane rides awaited me, bringing me first to Vancouver from Toronto, then across the Pacific Ocean to Taiwan, and finally to Kuala Lumpur. On my arrival there, I knew immediately I was in a different world. I was shocked by the flight attendant's casual statement that anyone found in possession of any type of narcotic would be sentenced to death. A final, quick hop then took me directly to Padang, capital of Sumatra. Though small, the airport was modern in many respects. I was struck by the customs officials' determination to secure their bribes before allowing me to get my entrance visa, but I was equally determined not to exchange dirty money for something I should receive by legitimate means. Eventually, they got tired of waiting, and I got my visa and baggage.

As I struggled to make my way with all my baggage through the throngs of people in the arrival hall, I looked for my host. Albert had said he would be waiting for me, but I didn't see him anywhere. After dodging several over-eager taxi drivers, I noticed a beautiful young Indonesian lady holding a curly-haired Caucasian boy. "Dr. Marcone?" she asked in her distinctive Indonesian accent "I am Albert's wife, Anita. I am here to pick you up." We exchanged a handshake and I followed her obediently through the masses of people in the airport terminal.

We got into a van and Anita explained to me that Albert was at home with some friends who were about to return to Australia. After about a twenty-minute ride, we arrived at an attractive, well-built home, clearly at the top of the market in the neighbourhood. I stepped out of the vehicle and made my way from the courtyard to the front door. Albert came out to greet me with a great big smile and a wonderful welcome that he repeated over and over again in his pleasant Australian accent.

My journey into the unknown had only just begun. I had finally met my carefully cultivated contacts in person. These were the people to whom I would entrust the final outcome of my work, and, ultimately, my safety and my life.

I spoke with three of Albert's friends, who, to my surprise, knew about my work on Kopi Luwak and had seen the television clip that appeared on the Discovery Channel's *Daily Planet* program. I explained to them that my research trip was aimed at trying to understand the secrets behind the low bacterial counts of Kopi Luwak coffee and its history. They said Albert had already given them their first taste of Kopi Luwak, and I was intrigued by their enthusiastic endorsements. As Albert had boasted that his was the real Kopi Luwak, they were quite interested in my observations.

They kept asking me if Kopi Luwak was truly worth six hundred dollars per pound and if I thought it was the best coffee in the world. I skirted the discussion, knowing that Albert was in earshot and wanting to hear what *they* thought.

Albert quickly stepped up to the plate with his candid analysis of the coffee. He indicated that the flavour of Kopi Luwak very much depended upon how and when it was collected and what drying method was used. Albert was quite insistent on this, and said he was eager to show me that the variations in flavour and quality of the Kopi Luwak currently available prevented its being designated the best coffee on the international market.

Then, springing to his feet, Albert said he would make me a cup, but that I would need to distinguish it from a control cup he would also brew for me. I agreed, and Anita walked to the back room and returned with two containers of coffee beans which she ground in two separate coffee grinders on their front counter. After the two cups of coffee were brewed, they were both presented to me and I got to work. In one of the cups, which I identified as the Kopi Luwak, the chocolaty overtone I had earlier discovered to be a defining characteristic of the coffee was quite evident, but the earthy and musty overtones were barely perceptible. Albert was impressed by my choice. He went on to say that my previous work on the coffee was evident, as most people would find it difficult to differentiate between the two cups. Under Albert's guidance I was to learn that the earthy and musty overtones I had thought were characteristic of Kopi Luwak were indicative of the relative quality of the particular batch of beans.

In what seemed to be a sudden change of topic, one of Albert's friends asked me if I limited my work to examining food delicacies such as Kopi Luwak coffee and the like, or if I also studied more common foods. Albert quickly interjected that he had seen television clips of me talking about a wide variety of different foods, including more "ordinary," everyday foods. It occurred to me that Albert knew much more about me than I had thought, which, quite frankly, caught me a little off guard. A bit unsettled, I refocused on Albert's friend and replied that I had worked on many types of foods for national television, and that my most recent project had been to determine the caffeine levels of popular coffees sold across Canada and the United States. I explained that CTV *National News* and *Canada AM* wanted to know the reason for the increased levels of caffeine in our coffee and the possible impact on public health. The news programs were particularly interested in learning if this was a wilful act on the part of the coffee companies aimed at getting people addicted to coffee, thereby increasing their sales, similar to the allegations that cigarette companies added extra nicotine to their cigarettes to keep people addicted. Albert again interjected, saying that he would like to see people getting hooked on Kopi Luwak coffee so that it would increase his sales!

"Nice try, Albert," I blurted out as everyone started laughing, including Albert. "In fact," I stated, "people can form a coffee habit but not a true addiction to coffee, as caffeine is a different sort of drug stimulant." What I did find is that coffee establishments were using coffee blends with higher levels of robusta coffee beans, which, although inferior to arabica coffee beans, were less expensive and therefore helped to stabilize retail coffee prices. But this price benefit had the unfortunate effect of dramatically increasing the amount of caffeine in the coffee, as robusta beans contain twice the level of caffeine of their arabica counterparts. Another of Albert's friends commented that he thought people were simply drinking more espressos and cappuccinos, which he believed contain more caffeine than ordinary coffee. They were all surprised to learn that a one-ounce espresso and a ten-ounce cup of coffee contain exactly the same amount of caffeine, the only difference being the concentration of caffeine in each beverage; in the end, each would deliver exactly the same punch.

Albert's friend, now visibly becoming more interested, pointed out that the coffee grounds used for espresso were darker and therefore must be higher in caffeine than regular coffee grounds. To this I replied that, while many people believe this to be true, test results show that darker-roasted coffee contains *less* caffeine than lighter roasts. The longer roasting times reduce the amount of caffeine.

The coffee conversation continued. During its course, all of Albert's friends concurred that coffee consumption was harmful to one's health—an unfortunate "evil" in today's fast-paced lifestyles. "Not so," I replied, "science tells another story." It has been shown scientifically that moderate coffee consumption (less than four hundred milligrams, or three cups, of coffee per day) actually delays the onset of Parkinson's disease and Type 2 diabetes in later years. Coffee is not as bad as was once thought, and actually may have beneficial properties for certain people with a predisposition to certain diseases. But while moderate coffee consumption can be beneficial, beverages containing high levels of caffeine can be harmful. Unfortunately, consumer demand has spurred the food industry to develop highly caffeinated beverages such as pop, "sport" drinks, and beer. This is where I, as a food scientist, have used the media to warn the public against their appetite for caffeinated products.

One of Albert's friends objected that I had just finished saying that caffeine might be good for people in small doses. I told him that I agreed with him, and stood behind my previous statement, but that caffeine was now showing up in beverages that are favourites among young people; these drinks never had caffeine in them prior to the current craze. While parents would not allow their ten-year-old to drink a cup of coffee, the same child can buy certain sodas at the store that contain one-and-a-half times the safe level of caffeine for someone that age. Too much caffeine can lead to problems in sleeping, as well as to behavioural and attention deficit problems in school. Furthermore, caffeine is an appetite suppressant, which can lead already picky eaters to consume less food or the wrong types of foods.

"As you can see," I concluded, "my television work is quite difficult at times due to the complexity of the issues surrounding what we eat."

Albert then asked, "On the topic of complexity, what do you think of my Kopi Luwak coffee that I prepared for you and which is now growing cold as we are trying to solve the world's problems?" I laughed and told Albert that he needed to make another set of coffees so we could continue to solve global problems. Anyway, these coffees were now cold and well past their prime. Albert grumbled in a funny sort of way and set off to make me a fresh, hot set of his precious brew.

As I once again sampled these coffees, Albert informed me that Detlef and his wife Nunu, two German television journalists, were on their way from the airport. They were to go with me into the rainforest to look for the luwak and the coffee it produced. No sooner had Albert said this than a car pulled up and the two journalists walked through the door. They approached me and shook my hand vigorously. They had just travelled from South Africa on a documentary filming expedition.

I was shocked to learn that our trip in search of the Kopi Luwak coffee in the rainforests of northern Sumatra had to begin under the cover of night. Much to my surprise and consternation, I was told that travelling at night was the only way to protect me from corrupt officials seeking to obstruct my research and modern-day highway robbers looking to make a buck.

The roads that led out of Padang were not very comfortable, and it seemed that whenever we picked up any speed we had to stop again to let people through or to manoeuvre around all the trucks leaving the city. Once free of the city, we moved along at a much steadier pace. At one point Albert turned to the two journalists and myself and asked if anyone had a GPS. He did not want us to take any coordinates or to reveal the location to which he was taking us. As a scientist, I had never considered myself a threat and had always prided myself on my ethics, so I was a bit taken aback by this blunt request. When nobody produced a GPS, Albert said he was just kidding, but I knew he had been serious.

Crossing the equator to the north was exciting. It felt as though we were moving into a different world. As we passed police officers making stops, Albert made sure that the only people who could be seen were our driver and Albert's father-in-law, who were both native Indonesians. He explained that an Australian, a German, an Ethiopian, and a Canadian would arouse suspicions. Overly interested police officers were not our only concern, though. Albert was visibly nervous about possible landslides that could block our route into northern Sumatra. Not only were these a safety concern, but any delay they occasioned could leave us at the mercy of the dishonest authorities who preyed upon people all over this route.

Just before one o'clock in the morning, the traffic came to a sudden stop and an uneasy silence descended over the vehicle. What was the delay? I wondered. Were we being stopped by the police? Ten minutes went by and traffic started to move again at a very slow pace. We veered off into the lane of oncoming traffic, inching ever so slowly forward until our headlights revealed the debris from a small landslide that had rolled down the mountainside and unceremoniously occupied a major portion of the roadway. Water and mud flowed down from the hillside, making it even more difficult to see where the debris ended and the road started. We kept edging farther over to the right, until I could see that our wheels were just inches from going over the escarpment. I nervously shouted out to Albert to be careful, lest we go over the side and plunge to our deaths in the darkness of the night. Albert, in a nervous but controlled voice, told me not to look as he had everything under control. He informed me that as a ship's captain he was prepared for any eventuality and that this would be no different just because we were on dry ground. Albert was confident—I was anything but!

Slowly, we moved further ahead, my heart pounding all the more as I waited for us to roll off the side of the escarpment. Finally, our wheels spun faster and we were catapulted forward, clear of the rocks, mud, trees, and other assorted things that tumbled down into the darkness. Albert turned to me; his face covered in sweat, and asked how I was doing. I told him I had been praying all the way and, thanks to God, my prayers had been answered. I looked behind me and noticed that Nunu and Detlef were sleeping in the back seat, totally oblivious to what had just occurred.

We made it through the night, sleeping only an hour and continuing our journey at three in the morning. After a few more hours we entered the area known as Mandheling where the Dutch settlers first established their coffee plantations centuries ago. Coffee trees, abandoned for decades, dotted the steep slopes, and I could only wonder who planted them and drank their coffee. Many of the trees were extremely old, their trunks twisted and gnarled. Very small paths were just barely visible, weaving through the coffee trees.

I noted that the trees were arabica and that the robusta coffee bushes were a more recent addition to the landscape. I could also see that the quality of today's Sumatran Mandheling coffee was due in part to the trees' position in the shade of the rainforest. Shade-grown coffee is known to be of much higher quality than coffee grown in full sun (plantation-grown) as the shade is believed to have an effect on the coffee similar to that of higher altitudes. The slower growth of the coffee beans results in the production of higher levels of "sugars" and other chemicals responsible for the beverage's perceived acidity. I wondered about the creative and observant people who had first noticed the difference in the shade-grown coffee.

Growing coffee under the shade of the forest trees was quite a common practice as it served many varied functions. While protecting the rainforest from being cut down, it also preserved the habitat of many migratory birds. As well, the trees bound the soil and provided shade for other shade-loving plants. Most importantly, however, the shade-grown coffee simply tasted better.

Finally, we had reached the land of the luwak, or palm civet. I had shed my distinctive white lab coat for camouflage, mystery, and subterfuge in the dead of night. I could barely contain my excitement, and my work had only just begun. We stopped in a village just before the area that we were going to survey. I was strictly instructed to keep the darkened windows closed so that the people in the village could not see who had arrived. My host exited the vehicle, spoke to the village chief at the corner, and requested permission for the vehicle to pass. A handshake, and we were off along the narrow dirt roads, heading into a semi-abandoned plantation. The rest of the journey would be on foot. I grabbed my belongings, my notebook and my research kit, and made my way deeper into the rainforest.

Eventually, we reached the spot that would be our home for the next several days. There, we would search for the Kopi Luwak coffee and the animal responsible for it—the creature they call the phantom. The ground was wet and covered with vegetation varying from grasses to broadleaf vines that travelled several feet along the ground before climbing up a tree, all in a quest to reach the light above. The ground was also covered with all sorts of fallen trees that had died or been cut down by the occasional person travelling through the forest. The decomposing trunks were the substrate for all sorts of fern-like vegetation and tiny flowering plants that clung to their sides and bark.

Lifting my head, I could see a deep ravine covered in fog that was just beginning to lift. It was one of the most beautiful landscapes I had ever seen. I stared for a few minutes, the breeze blowing away parts of the fog and exposing more of the scenery below. It seemed that this moment had been made for me. It was magnificent! I heard the call of the gibbons in the distance, and Albert walked up to me and said that this was his paradise, his favourite part of the rainforest. He encouraged me to enjoy it and to learn from the secrets that it contained.

My new home and laboratory was a rickety old shack whose thin walls and roof barely succeeded in keeping out the daily rain. A small gasoline feed generator provided our electricity, and the rain was our only source of drinking water. My heretofore "indispensable" modern conveniences such as showers and toilets were non-existent.

Shortly after nightfall, the dogs announced the arrival of a visitor. There at the door stood the village chief whom we had seen earlier in the day. In his hand he held the leg of a wild deer caught earlier in the day and this was to be our evening meal. I took the leg, still covered with the brown fur of the recently slaughtered animal, examining it with the eyes of a scientist and the same skepticism that I would have brought to bear in my laboratory thousands of kilometres away. But this was my dinner, so I put aside my scruples.

That evening we skinned the fur off the deer's leg and carefully cut the bush meat into thin slices so we could fry it in a pan with a little oil that Albert had brought with him. Our cooking facilities were rather primitive and crude, but sufficed to prepare our foods during our brief interlude in the rainforest. Just outside the shack that protected us from the torrential rains was a shelter for the wood we had collected from the forest floor and left piled up to dry. A special elevated fire-pit was all we had on which to cook our food. Whenever we cooked, smoke would fill our sleeping quarters.

Night was a time to relax and regain the strength that we had lost. My bed was a mere few boards nailed together, and I slept in my clothes in case I was disturbed during the night. Flashlight in hand, I began to sleep, only to be awakened by a rat crawling over me. With a shout, I got up from my bed in disbelief, thinking that this could not have happened to me. This was not my first, nor my last, encounter with the rodents that inhabited this shack, and I was struck by the role reversal from my encounters with rats back home. There, researchers controlled lab rats. Here, the rats were in charge, and I was merely an observer as they attacked each other, once even fighting under my bed.

As the sun rose on our little shack, revealing the rainforest in its luscious splendour, I wondered if the luwak had left any treasures for me to collect and analyze. With great anticipation, I quickly ate my breakfast of cereal mixed with UHT milk (milk treated to be stable without the need for refrigeration). A few days later, when I discovered that the cereal I was eating was infested with some kind of microscopic ant, my breakfast quickly changed to a variety of locally collected fruits. Interestingly, my encounter with ants would not end here but would follow me back to North America (Mexico) where what I thought was absurd in Indonesia became another adventure in rare food delicacies: ant egg caviar.

I walked down the slopes of green hills covered so thickly with shrubs and vines that they obscured the ground. The earth was fertile, brown and rich, covered with leaves and decaying matter of all kinds. The vegetation was quite dense in places, making progress difficult. The moisture on the ground made everything extremely slippery, and we had to watch our every step to avoid falling down the steep embankments. The vegetation glimmered with tiny droplets from the previous night's rainfall. Each droplet had a way of catching the light that streamed through the canopy above and reflecting it in every direction. I was instructed to keep my arms completely covered and to wear my wide-brimmed pith helmet at all times while in the forest as there were tiny leeches in the rain droplets on the vegetation throughout the area.

I was frequently struck in the head by branches that had been bent forward by those travelling in front of me. If it had not been for the unique construction of my pith helmet, the hike would have been unbearable. The helmet was light yet rigid, and had good ventilation. I marvelled to think that the explorers of the past had used a similar hat during their travels throughout rainforests and jungles around the world. I guess certain things are made to survive the passage of time. It is amazing how important such a seemingly insignificant item was—not only having it but also its engineering. Before my journey it would never have occurred to me to value my pith helmet so highly.

A group of coffee harvesters guided us through the old plantation, indicating possible locations to find the Kopi Luwak coffee. We were told to observe closely where trees had fallen, for this was prime luwak real estate. The luwak habitually deposited its treasure around rocks and tree stumps, in elevated and sunken areas. In some locations the luwak's coffee had escaped the collector's eye, and in its place lay a clump of coffee seedlings. This was a very interesting finding as it indicated that the surface pitting and interior protein breakdown I had noted in the laboratory were not destructive to the bean. It appeared that the civet was Mother Nature's way of distributing coffee plants across a wide geographical area. The civet's appetite for this coffee cherry is a very important part of nature's delicate web and was a guarantee that the coffee plant, although not native to Indonesia, would still be distributed far and wide

Later on in the laboratory and in my research greenhouse at the university, I discovered that the passage of coffee beans through the civet not only reduced their germination time by 50 percent but also increased the number of beans that would germinate. Thirty percent more of the coffee beans that had gone through the civet's GI tract germinated as compared with those from the collected control samples. The beans' short and uneventful journey through the civet's GI tract is actually beneficial and critical to their germination rates, and hence to their survival. In other words, this "special" relationship was important for the survival of both the creature and the plant, a mutually beneficial relationship not uncommon in nature. A collector's shout brought me running. I could hardly contain my excitement, and was barely able to prevent myself from falling as I made my way through the thick vegetation. The steepness of the incline made it even more difficult for me to keep my balance as I manoeuvred around the dead stumps on the ground below. I finally made it to the collector, who signalled me to the exact location. He pulled the vegetation back to give me a better look at the treasure I had travelled around the world to find and so longed to see.

There it lay, a freshly deposited clump of Kopi Luwak coffee...it was beautiful! It was during the night that had just passed, as the rainforest rats were robbing me of my precious sleep, that the luwak had left a surprise gift for me to find. A million questions raced through my mind. What should I do first? Photograph it? Survey the area around it? Collect a sample of it? I resisted the urge to gloat over my new-found treasure, and took my time approaching the pile as a scientist. No one rushed me as I took my measurements and samples. This was future evidence for me as well as for others to show that Kopi Luwak coffee was not an urban legend or myth as some had thought, but that the tales about its origins were in fact true in every respect. And I was the one collecting the data that would put the record straight. The collectors then led me to other found piles of Kopi Luwak, from which I also collected data and samples.

Now that we had fresh samples in hand, Albert showed me the differences he had mentioned earlier, at his home in Padang. He showed me that piles of Kopi Luwak were slightly different in colour, some lighter and some a little darker and slightly drier. He indicated that the darker and slightly drier piles were ones that had missed the collectors' eyes and had therefore stayed longer on the forest floor. According to Albert, these piles would begin to ferment after the first day, producing a coffee of inferior quality with regard to both aroma and taste. For the best Kopi Luwak flavour and aroma, he insisted, the coffee scats (as they are called) had to be collected as soon as possible after being deposited. Unfortunately, many Kopi Luwak collectors had no systematic method of collection, which led to variations in the quality of the coffee on the market. Albert showed me how he had divided Kopi Luwak into three distinct grades, which he collected separately and processed in different ways. We would test these three grades in our shack that evening.

On my own, I went deeper and deeper into the rainforest, asking Detlef and Nunu to follow me. I made my own discoveries of Kopi Luwak scats, to avoid being led to find specific scats; this way I was sure they were absolutely real. At various points I collected more samples. Each scat contained approximately two hundred coffee beans, which would indicate the civet ate approximately a hundred cherries per day. A quick calculation showed that one could get approximately three cups of coffee per scat. What a picture—three cups of brew from each pile of civet excrement!

That evening, we used the generator to power a small roaster I had brought from Canada, and we roasted the day's find of Kopi Luwak coffee, which had been washed, prepared, and dried by the collectors. The aroma of roasted coffee filled the shack and emanated from our location like incense. Hopefully, the luwak could sense that we had transformed his treasure into something that was infinitely appreciated and valued.

Albert brought forth the various grades of Kopi Luwak he had collected and prepared. We carefully roasted them and evaluated each cup. It soon became evident to me that Albert was correct: the coffee that had remained longer on the forest floor lacked the full body and acidity that the freshly collected coffee possessed. I saw that a methodology for collecting these scats was essential in order to grade each collected pile.

That night, I lay in bed wondering about all that I had seen and heard. As the gibbons' howls dissipated, along with the rainforest's usual sounds, I knew that many questions still remained unanswered.

The next day, I was brought up a steep hill to an area set aside to prepare the freshly collected Kopi Luwak for drying. The buckets of Kopi Luwak coffee were brought to a basin area with a metal screen over the bottom. The coffee was dumped into the bottom and water was poured over the beans as they were vigorously scrubbed. The reason for the lower bacterial counts now became clear. The washing and scrubbing of the beans would remove a substantial amount of the bacteria on the bean surface. The carbohydrate used by bacteria to adhere to various surfaces would be loosened and removed during this energetic procedure. This was a fantastic finding, and one of the important objectives of my visit to the rainforest. Now I understood why the bacterial counts were consistently lower for Kopi Luwak beans (although they were picked out of feces) compared with their controls: many of the bacteria had been simply scrubbed away.

All at once it struck me that this procedure would also explain the unusual homogeneity of the bacterial colonies on the Kopi Luwak plates as compared with the controls. During washing, certain types of bacteria would be more susceptible to being washed off, leaving other (but fewer) types still clinging to the beans. This phenomenon, combined with the types of competitive exclusions—the behaviour of some of the bacteria in the intestinal flora of the civet that limited the types of bacteria colonizing in the intestine—explained my unusual results.

When we finally packed our bags for the return to Padang, we travelled again under the cover of night. After we crossed the equator, a uniformed police officer ran out to the road to pull us over. We knew his purpose was extortion rather than a legitimate stop, so our driver sped away. As we did so, I noticed that our extorter then decided to stop the vehicle directly behind us, much to our surprise. The fear this incident inspired stayed with me for quite a while. I was sure we would be pulled over at any moment for bypassing a checkpoint, but we arrived safely.

I could only marvel at the contrast between Albert's house in Padang and the shack we had left behind in the rainforest only eight hours previously. Albert was quick to get us settled in so that we could all get a good night's rest. Before we went to bed, Albert showed me a room in his house that contained baskets upon baskets of coffee with various labels affixed to them. This was the only room in the entire house that was air-conditioned, with the humidity strictly controlled, an indication of the value of the room's contents. This was where the many pounds of Kopi Luwak coffee collected from the rainforest were kept to finish its drying process. I was amazed when I considered the journey this coffee had made and would soon make to grace the tables of the elite few around the world privileged enough to be able to afford it.

The next day, we boarded a plane for a one-hour flight to the island of Java, and the capital of Indonesia, Jakarta. When we arrived, Detlef and Nunu informed me that we needed to go to the Ministry of Information to get the permits to film the documentary on Kopi Luwak in Indonesia. I turned to them in surprise and asked why we had been filming in Sumatra without a permit. They indicated that they had had preliminary permission from the Indonesian embassy in Belgium, but that they needed full permission in order to complete the rest of the work. I was a little confused at this point, but decided not to pursue this matter as I really did not know what the rules were (nor, frankly, did I want to know).

At the Ministry of Information, we made our way to the sixth floor to meet the various officials in charge of permitting procedures. I was asked by the undersecretary of the ministry why I wanted to film a documentary about this coffee and about their country. I explained the whole story of my involvement in the project, candidly stating that I had previously doubted the validity of the story behind Kopi Luwak. The undersecretary smiled at me and said that many even in Indonesia believed the same thing, but that my recent findings about Kopi Luwak were in keeping with the information he and his ministry possessed. He explained how his relatives in the outskirts of Jakarta collected and brewed this coffee when he was a child. He went on to say that it was the Western world that created such a demand for it due to what was perceived to be an odd production process. He was quick to add that this was a natural way of collecting coffee for further brewing and he did not see anything odd about it, nor did he understand the West's fascination with it.

We were given our permits and told that, while filming in Jakarta, we needed to have an information officer with us at all times. Filming near military installations was strictly forbidden, as were filming in Atjeh province in Sumatra and in Sulawesi, due to the civil war that was occurring there.

With permits in hand, we left the Ministry of Information and made our way to see another contact. Alun was another expatriate, from New Zealand, and had set up a coffee roasting business in Jakarta. Detlef, Nunu, and I met with him and asked if we could speak with some native people about Kopi Luwak. Also, could Alun arrange for us to see one of the civets who were responsible for this coffee?

Alun called his wife and told her to meet us at the Jakarta animal market. When we got there, Lisa and Nunu disappeared for a short while and then came back saying they had spoken to an animal trader with a captive civet. My sense of justice rebelled at the thought of trapping wild animals to meet man's unfounded demand for them. Nunu understood my outrage, but said that in Indonesia the government had decided to allow these markets to continue as many of these animals were eaten by the locals. In any case, she said, the government was unable to control the trade in animals.

We approached the market tents. The trader asked twenty dollars for the palm civet, (*Parodoxurus hermapheoditus*) which Nunu paid, and the cage was given to her. Thus, on the outskirts of Jakarta, I first came face to face with the palm civet, the animal that I had travelled halfway around the world to study. Ours was a friendly six-month-old youngster that quickly made itself comfortable when we picked it up. At maturity, this animal weighs between 2–6 kilograms with a long (43–71 cm) slender body, short legs

45

and a long tail (41–66 cm). The Indonesians affectionately call it a toddy cat, as it likes to drink the sweet palm sap. Toddy is an Indonesian spirit made from palm sap. Here I observed for the very first time my elusive little friend, and the unsuspecting participant in the making of Kopi Luwak coffee. The palm civet had evaded me during my visit to the rainforest, leaving only its scattered coffee scats for me to find. Now the cat-and-mouse game was over, and I had not only set eyes on the mysterious little creature but had him in the palm of my hand! As I was cradling this wild, tree-living "cat," it was hard to believe that this tiny creature was the maker of the world's most expensive coffee...so much from so little! I held the civet close to my heart and could feel it snuggling into me. It was a most beautiful moment... finally to meet the animal for which I had travelled halfway around the world to study...we had now been officially introduced! I wanted to release it and allow it to return to its natural habitat but was told that this would mean imminent death for my new friend as he would surely be caught again and end up at the same animal market for resale... and who knows what his fate would then be? Alun told me that he would keep him in the backyard sanctuary along with many other animals he had rescued from a similar fate.

Later, we had the opportunity to visit an old village in the nearby valley where coffee had been grown for as long as anyone could remember. The people here were not plantation owners but made their livelihoods collecting and processing coffee for the landowners, who would then export it to various countries. The homes were basically one- or two-room shacks, but they were very well maintained. Alun, although he spoke perfect Indonesian, had difficulty communicating with these people, but his wife Lisa was very well versed in this specific dialect. During the course of our conversations we asked many questions about Kopi Luwak. Surprisingly, we were informed by these people that they often collected this coffee for their own consumption and that their personal stores were not for sale. They told me that since they did not own the coffee field, the coffee they picked did not belong to them; but, according to local custom, anything that was on the ground could be taken by the finder. Then it struck me: the first people to collect and drink Kopi Luwak coffee were only doing what local custom allowed them to do, namely, take and consume what did not belong to anyone else. These generations of coffee collectors were not people who brewed up coffee retrieved from cat feces on a dare, but people who used their ingenuity to solve a problem.

Forty-eight hours after I left the island on December 22, a tsunami claimed the lives of 216,000 people. The event shocked me to the very core. As I sat motionless, transfixed in front of the television on Boxing Day morning, 2004, I felt fear return—the same fear that had gripped me when I had first contemplated my journey to Indonesia. What surprised me was that, while I had mostly feared a terrorist attack by al Qaeda, like the one they had orchestrated in Bali in 2002, the attack I had just barely escaped had come from Mother Nature herself. The tsunami had inflicted a far greater number of deaths and more terror and fear than any man-made attack could possibly have done. I was truly heartbroken to see that people with whom I had spent time and had adventures, people who had shared their food and homes with me, people who had guided me safely through the jungle and protected me from so many dangers, should suffer such a catastrophic blow. I tried contacting Albert, and after three days I was finally able to reach him. He and his family were fine, but many people he had known had died while others had lost the little they owned. While I made it home safe and sound, some of my luggage did not. In the total devastation and confusion after the tsunami, some of my luggage with samples more precious than gold were misplaced and not found for months. By this time, the samples were moldy, ruined and lost. Fortunately I had taken duplicate samples with me on the plane. They were now safe and sound in my lab, not in the original quantity—but I was safe, even if my Indonesian friends were not. God bless them.

Later, I asked my pastor why nature had inflicted such a blow on the people of Indonesia. He simply replied, "Nature never forgives, man sometimes forgives, but God always forgives." He did not need to elaborate. Truly, I had met all three on my adventures—nature, man, and God!

ETHIOPIA

IN SEARCH FOR AN ALTERNATIVE SOURCE OF
KOPI LUWAK COFFEE

While my Indonesian adventure had answered many of my questions about Kopi Luwak coffee, it also whetted my appetite to learn more about this strange brew. Not long after my return to Canada, I received a call from a young entrepreneur named Blake who wanted to start importing Kopi Luwak to North America. He was very much interested in exploring other potential sources as the Kopi Luwak coffee was very rare and limited.

Since coffee beans are grown in more than eighty countries around the world, all of which lie within 1,600 kilometres north or south of the equator, we focused our search around the equator. A quick investigation of existing literature indicated that the Indonesian palm civet, the source of Kopi Luwak, did in fact have a close cousin, the African civet (*Civettictis civetta*). We began to investigate the African civet as a possible alternate producer for an African version of Kopi Luwak coffee.

The African civet, weighing between seven and twenty kilograms, is known to live in sub-Saharan Africa along a stretch from Senegal to Somalia, and also in Namibia and eastern South Africa. This stretch lies right within the aforementioned 1,600-kilometre coffee belt. Unlike the Indonesian civet, the African variety lives mainly on the ground in forests, savannahs, and similar areas with long grasses and thickets. It typically inhabits areas near permanent water systems and has the reputation of being a good swimmer. Both civets are nocturnal, depending on their acute sense of smell to find food. And both deposit their feces in special piles called civetries (naturally constructed "litter boxes"), located near the edges of their territory.

Interestingly, we also discovered that for centuries the Ethiopians have captured and housed this animal and harvested the musk from its perineal glands located just underneath the tail. This musk has traditionally been used to make perfume, but that use has been greatly reduced due to the intervention of animal rights activists. Because at its relative political stability and long history of growing quality arabica coffee, Ethiopia became our target, and we planned a research expedition into that country in December when the coffee cherries start to ripen.

We made arrangements to meet with local Ethiopians to search for the African civet to determine if it also consumed coffee. If this type of civet did in fact consume coffee, would the beans excreted produce a brew similar to the world-famous Indonesian Kopi Luwak? Packing my sample containers and laboratory equipment, I felt like an explorer venturing into dangerous and uncharted territory. In a sense, I was: so far as I knew, I was the first food scientist to search the region for a new food source.

After an exhausting twenty-four hours of airplane hopping, I finally arrived a few days ahead of Blake in Addis Ababa, the capital of Ethiopia. With the second-highest elevation of any national capital, the air in Addis Ababa was very thin—a fact that was evident every time I climbed a flight of stairs. Unlike my trip to Indonesia, this time I had made sure to get my visa back in Canada to avoid unnecessary bureaucratic hassles. A quick stamp of the passport admitted me into the country, and I was ready to start my work. Where the eager Indonesian taxi drivers were unfazed by late arrival times, here the late hour meant that there were fewer taxis available to take me to my destination, and I had to share one with a couple who had also just arrived. The driver packed in our luggage and had to tie the trunk closed as it was loaded to the very top and spilling over. Our combined weight made the car sink noticeably, almost hugging the road surface.

The driver spoke little English but this did not matter as long as he could take us to our respective hotels. First to be dropped off were the couple, whose hotel seemed to be within walking distance of the airport. My hotel, on the other hand, was not. The old taxi was in a dubious state of repair and stalled while going up a steep hill. Unfortunately, this would not be my last experience with Ethiopian vehicles that were not roadworthy. Indeed, the taxi was a complete and utter wreck, and it was amazing that it held together and could actually move! Once it started up, it shook uncontrollably like a ship tossed on rough seas, and threatened to stall again at any moment. Both the oil indicator and the alternator lights kept flashing insistently. "Pay attention to us," they seemed to say—but they were ignored. "There is more wrong with this vehicle than right," I thought to myself as the driver encouraged the car forward. The seats were as worn as the motor, the upholstery shredded and the padding non-existent. I could feel the seat springs digging into my legs and back with every shake, rattle, and roll along the road to my hotel. Welcome to Addis Ababa, Ethiopia!

I watched the driver grow more and more nervous as we went along, and noticed that he did not appear to know exactly how to get to my hotel. When we began driving down a series of abandoned streets, I started to become extremely nervous. I clutched my money belt and passport and wondered if I was to be mugged, or worse. After ten minutes of driving through those dangerous areas, we finally made it to a lighted street, and there I saw the hotel sign. Glad to be alive, I sprang out of the taxi and paid the driver the predetermined fare. I was met at the door of the hotel by the guard, who wore a very long trench coat that went well below his knees, and a woollen scarf around his head and neck. The evening was cold, which was in part due to our extremely high elevation.

When Blake finally arrived after a few days, we proceeded to obtain permission from the Ethiopian Wildlife Organization (EWO) to search for the elusive African civet. Dealing with the organization was most interesting, but in many ways extremely frustrating. I knew right away that I could not depend on the conservation authorities, so we would be on our own. With this in mind, we visited the Ethiopian Coffee and Tea Authority (ECTA) to glean information about the various coffee-rich areas. I was given an official tour of the facilities and saw for myself how coffee was processed through the port. I was astounded at the sheer volume of coffee that passed through this facility each and every day.

Upon arrival at the port, the coffee was cleaned by removing foreign matter of all sorts, including leaves, twigs, sticks, pebbles, stones, metal, and ropes, among other things. The metal was removed with strong magnetic equipment. The coffee was then divided into a multitude of different streams by both air and gravity separators, with only the highest quality being released for export; the inferior grades were kept for local consumption. It struck me as ironic and sad that the people inhabiting the country whence this coveted product originated centuries upon centuries ago would only consume the poorest grades of it.

After observing the cleaning and separation processes, I was given a tour and further instructions on the official coffee-cupping procedure used to grade Ethiopian coffee. The quality-testing facility had literally thousands of cups (bowls) of coffee at various stages of testing.

At the end I was given a map of all the coffee regions of Ethiopia, indicating, as well, all the different possible locations to find the civet. Armed with this information our driver, Abebe, and I mapped out our expedition; and so we began a 2,700-kilometre journey through some of the remotest regions of Ethiopia in a 1996 Land Cruiser carrying sixty litres of spare fuel on its roof, two spare tires, and a jerry can containing twenty litres of water. I was very pleased to know that Abebe was an experienced safari guide and well acquainted with the remote areas of southern Ethiopia. Thankfully, his knowledge would not only keep us safe, but would also help us track down the African civet. Evidently, this animal, in addition to being nocturnal, was elusive and ferocious by nature.

Our vehicle was not only our mode of transportation but also our protection from the elements. The roadways were so dusty that our hair and everything else in the vehicle became completely blackened with dust by the end of day. Blowing one's nose quickly showed how much dust we were inhaling, and cleaning out the vehicle became a necessary daily ritual. The Land Cruiser also served as a barrier between us and the crowds of people on the roads and in the villages, who acted as though the circus had come to town. Much to my surprise, Abebe said that the regions we were visiting were so remote and unconnected to the outside world that I may have been the first white person some of these people had ever seen, especially the youngest ones. Whenever I left the vehicle, children followed me around as though I were some kind of celebrity. They would pull the hair on my arms in amazement, comment on my white skin, and point out to one another the braces on my teeth. One inquisitive little boy even asked me if my skin would become the same colour as his. The constant scrutiny was a bit unsettling, and I wondered how past explorers must have felt.

Our entire journey was so dogged by minor catastrophes that I felt like a cross between Dr. Livingstone and Mr. Magoo. Flat tires and broken clutches seemed to occur at the most inopportune times. The rough, unpaved, and badly maintained roads required us to stop several times a day to adjust the clutch. Even when the vehicle was totally functional, the mud would hold us back and we were ever grateful for Abebe's resourcefulness. Travelling through southern Ethiopia was like journeying through a never-ending dust bowl. The only reprieves from the dust were our short stops to obtain supplies again, when we would enter one of the tiny restaurants that dotted the sides of the busy streets to enjoy a sojourn out of the blistering sun. We welcomed this relief from the oppressive heat that smothered us in our confined vehicle and caused the dust to stick to the beads of sweat appearing on every patch of exposed skin. These stops also offered a respite from the torture inflicted on us by the bumpy uneven roads, each bump seemingly being able to find a way to make us sore in new places.

Most of the buildings we saw were made of the same basic materials—mud, cow dung, and straw—which would be left to ferment for weeks in outdoor pools before being fashioned into bricks or used as plaster to cement the bricks together. During the rainy season, the buildings would slowly begin to deteriorate as the walls gradually absorbed the water and, quite literally, crumbled away. It was interesting that even the more sophisticated buildings were made of this material. For example, the building housing a city's telecommunications equipment, which was in many cases the community's only link to the outside world, was composed of the same cow-dung bricks as the local outhouse! You could spot these communications buildings from a distance by their towering steel antennas and large satellites; then, upon closer inspection, you saw that all the signals from this sophisticated equipment were being fed into a dung shack. Apparently, the people in Ethiopia looked for creative and practical ways to use *everything*, and cow dung was a very important and abundant resource. While our Western sensibilities might be somewhat revolted by the notion of buildings made of dung, the creativity and good sense of the people in finding ways to build shelter in a country with few suitable and readily available abundant building materials are commendable. Sometimes, though, this trip seemed to be all about feces. As I searched for Kopi Luwak coffee, the beans that were extracted from civet feces,

I stayed in huts made of cow dung. Thank God our jeep was not made of the same material!

This being said, I should note that the buildings were painted in such a way as to effectively disguise the composition of the walls. Some of the buildings even had the luxury of being wired for electricity; in these, a sole bare light bulb would illuminate the entire structure. But even though the building might be wired for electricity, this did not guarantee that electricity would always be available. In Ethiopia, electricity is as reliable as running water, which is to say when you need it the most, it's not available. And when it is available, it is shut down at ten o'clock every evening providing only a few precious hours of light during the intense darkness of the night. When we refuelled the vehicle and/or replenished our fuel reservoir, we often had to resort to using a manual hand pump as the electricity at gas stations was always in very short supply.

After a quick bite to eat, made even quicker by the lack of choice at the roadside restaurants, we would be back on our way in our bouncing jeep, the pain in our bruised muscles redoubling after the brief respite.

Despite the giant potholes and omnipresent dust, the thing that most disconcerted me were the thousands of cows sharing the road with us. And it was not only cows that were common road hazards and obstacles. We also observed but, more importantly, also avoided running into all manner of other critters—goats, donkeys, monkeys, large birds, and an assorted menagerie of other indiscernible farm animals. Many of the cows looked very old and all of them had huge horns, something that one does not customarily see in North America. These horns were used by the people as containers for various foods and drinks, as well as for carving various decorative items for roadside sale. I even bought a few for my family and friends at home. The cows rocked their heads from side to side to fan off the many flies that landed on them, and this motion made me very uneasy. I was always waiting for one of their horns to either pierce our radiator or come crashing through a car window, either of which would cause a major problem. There was no AAA or CAA to help us on our way.

Abebe informed me that these cows were very important in the Ethiopian diet. Ethiopians by nature are heavy meat eaters, and the *injeras*, or flatbreads that we typically ate, were heavily meat based. Abebe indicated that the tragic Ethiopian famine of the mid-1980s was the direct result of a drought that killed most of the cattle. After the death of the cattle, the Ethiopian people lost their main food sources: meat and milk, the latter also used for making cheese, became non-existent for most people. Millions of Ethiopians starved to death, particularly in the agriculture-poor coffee-growing areas to which we were headed. As the drought continued, it denied the few vegetables, fruits, and cattle fodder plants the much needed life-giving water, and many people died waiting for food aid. Abebe told me to say a prayer for the dead and two prayers for those who survived, that such a tragedy would never recur in his country or any other. Nature had been as unforgiving to the Ethiopian people as she had been to the hundreds of thousands of Indonesians who perished in the killer tsunami of Boxing Day, 2004. It appeared that these two countries' economic hardship over the years did not earn them any counterbalancing exemption from Mother Nature's worst attacks. I pondered once again what my pastor had told me, trying to make sense of it all.

Although the journey was slow and sometimes treacherous, the beauty of the landscape made it all worthwhile. The land was vast and varied. We travelled through everything from semi-arid areas to deciduous forests, from evergreen regions to savannah and rainforests. Never had I seen such a great diversity of landscapes in such a small geographical area. Each landscape had its own beauty and indigenous animals. We saw black-and-white colobus monkeys, dik-diks, zebras, kudus, gorillas, impalas, and a variety of Abyssinian birds, to name a few. I was particularly fascinated by the dik-diks. They looked like deer but were only about a foot-and-a-half tall. They mated for life and ran in groups of approximately thirty individuals. I saw that the books decrying Ethiopia's shortage of wildlife are outdated. The animals, although in many cases threatened in their natural environment, could still be seen on the sides of the road looking or foraging for food.

Our travels took us from the capital directly south to Arba Minch, a town located within a short two-hour drive from the Kenyan border. There the land was rich in natural resources but in many ways untouched due to the nature reserve that the Ethiopian government created many years ago. We spent the day going through that reserve, which provided numerous armed scouts to guide the visitors. Their role was to protect visitors from wild animals while at the same time acting as a deterrent to poachers.

I asked the driver to stop so I could photograph a herd of zebras grazing on the tall grasses in the near distance. As I approached them, I marvelled that they did not run away from me, but only observed albeit nervously. Soon I found myself among the zebras, with some only a mere five metres away! I slowly looked around, moving as little as possible, and saw in amazement that I had made my way into a herd of approximately seventy zebras. I carefully snapped a few photos of these majestic creatures and wondered in a silly sort of way if they were actually black with white stripes or white with black stripes.

Suddenly, the animals became agitated. They were looking nervously around from one place to another, their hooves striking the ground as if in defiance. As a group, they started to move in the direction of the sun. Just then, the scout called to me with a quite urgent tone in his voice... return to the vehicle. I made my way back, trying not to upset the zebras any further. As I got farther away from them and closer to the scout, he raised his voice, telling me several times to come back into the vehicle.

I wondered what was going on. Why were the zebras so agitated and why was the scout so insistent that I return to the vehicle? Being the only one who did not know what was happening made me uneasy. Upon my return to the vehicle, the scout said that the agitation we both had observed in the zebras was probably due to an Abyssinian lion that had made its way from the heights to the lower elevation where the zebras lived. The zebras had realized they might soon be under attack and started to reposition themselves to flee as a herd. It was only then that I realized that these huge, muscular creatures could have stampeded me during their escape, and that even if I had avoided this fate, the only thing between the zebras and the lion would have been me. With a silent chuckle, I thought how ironic it would be if a food scientist became food himself. The notion of being snacked on by a wild predator was not appealing in the least! I was looking for a small catlike creature that ate coffee— not a large one that ate people! At least I was safe in my Land Cruiser for the time being...or so I thought.

Not finding the civet in the savannahs around Arba Minch, we made our way back north to the capital, revisiting the various locations we had passed earlier. The wildlife authorities were as unhelpful as before, and so I turned to faith as my guide. I walked around the grounds of a local church and prayed to God, asking why He had brought me here if not to find the civet and to discover if it ate coffee cherries like its distant cousin in Indonesia. I knew then that there was a lot for me to learn in Ethiopia, a country that few would visit voluntarily. I knew that I had to learn patience and to live in the moment instead of looking down the road to see what was coming up.

A little disappointed, but in many ways relieved, I knew that God had answered my questions, even if the answers were not exactly what I had expected or wanted. I had to accept that, although I was conducting scientific research, my noble activities did not exempt me from life's problems and setbacks. Certain things in life are out of our control. I was confident, however, that God wanted me to continue and to trust Him in this adventure. I reminded myself that the word "research" is made up of two parts—"re" and "search." So what I needed to do was to search and then search again.

We journeyed from Addis Ababa southwest into the rich coffee-growing areas of Ethiopia, hoping that we could accomplish our goals without the assistance of those familiar with the area. In Jimma, where we encountered yet another unhelpful Ethiopian Wildlife Organization official, we happened to meet a member of the Ethiopian royal family that had ruled this area for centuries. He explained that Ethiopia had degenerated from a strong and powerful kingdom into a country plagued by war, famine, and disease. Meeting him was like a journey into history. We learned that Ethiopia was the only country in the whole of Africa that had never been colonized, and that this fact had allowed it to maintain many of its ancient traditions, one of which was the centuries-old practice of maintaining captive civets.

This gentleman told us to travel west towards Limu as this was an area known for both wild and captive civets. Going on nothing more than his recommendation, we made our way towards Limu. On the outskirts we met many farmers who actually owned civets that they had caught in the wild and raised in order to collect their musk. It is written in the Bible that the Queen of Sheba brought King Solomon a gift of musk when she visited his kingdom (1 Kings 10:1–13). Musk has been used as a perfume and as a medicinal drink for many centuries, and it continues to serve as an important ingredient in expensive European perfumes and colognes. The civetone in the musk makes the fragrance persist on the wearer's skin for a prolonged period of time. Unfortunately, the farmers were unwilling to let us see their animals because they believed our presence would distress and kill the civets. I was sharply reminded of Aztecs hiding their gold from Cortés.

We travelled north to Yanfa on steep roads so narrow that the Land Cruiser had to push aside tree branches in order to get through. When the road gradually disappeared, I was surprised to see young men approach us with spears in their hands. I was confused and frightened, but they only took us to an open area at the highest point on the hill where the village elders indicated to us where we could look for our civet, pointing from the hilltop into the far-off lands.

We made our way in the direction the elders had recommended to a location four-and-a-half hours away, reaching a place called Abdellah in the province of Illubabor. Abdellah consisted merely of a few mud-and-dung huts on the side of a narrow gravel road. None of the villagers with whom we spoke seemed to understand for what we were searching, but as we were about to leave, a man nervously approached the vehicle and spoke to our guide. Our guide informed us that this person had been collecting coffee one day when he saw a civet hiding in the thickets on the outskirts where the coffee was growing. We were excited and wondered if this could be our big break. The man agreed to take us to the spot, and I grabbed my supplies and camera and started to follow.

As the guide stayed behind to watch the vehicle and do some minor repairs, my safety was in the hands of a stranger. We walked for approximately thirty-five minutes through bushes and a variety of other plants to the location where he had seen the civet. By then, eight other individuals had collected around us, curious as to what we were after. I retold the story to all of them and they all agreed that they wanted to assist in surveying the area. They were instructed that if anything was found, it was not to be touched until I arrived.

We searched for approximately thirty minutes but it felt like an eternity. Then a voice called out and I made my way over to where three individuals squatted in the brush, looking at something on the ground. I was moved with emotion and excitement as I approached them. For a brief moment I was taken back to my first Kopi Luwak coffee find in the rainforest in Indonesia. Although this was not my first time finding the hidden treasures of the civet, my prior experience did not detract from the feelings of excited anticipation and anxiety that came over me now. While pushing the vegetation aside, I noted the differences between the rainforests of Indonesia and the deciduous and coniferous forests and savannahs of Ethiopia. These two locations were worlds apart, but each held secrets. They were so different...and yet so much the same.

And then, there it was—a freshly laid scat deposited by a civet!

It had the same spider shape as its Indonesian cousin's scat, confirming that the shape belonged exclusively to the civet. In fact, the shape was exactly the same as that of the scats I had seen in Indonesia, the only differences being that it was larger and much more organic in nature. Without disturbing the scat, I immediately took photos and measurements. In the vicinity I observed three or four mature coffee plants ripe with red coffee cherries, but they were distant enough that the cherries or their hidden coffee beans could not have fallen into the scat contaminating it. I put on my rubber gloves, standard apparel in a laboratory setting but totally abnormal in this type of environment, especially to the guides around me. I started to probe through the scat with a stick, taking samples of the hair and what appeared to be bone in the feces. Then something caught my eye. Could it be the coffee that I was looking for? I reached in and pulled it out. Here was the single coffee bean that I had travelled halfway around the world to find.

I was shocked, ecstatic, and shaking in awe of what I had found. I carefully put it into a sample bag, labelled it, and documented it in my laboratory data collection book. I dug further into the scat only to find another coffee bean and then another and another, for a grand total of ten. I concluded that I had fulfilled one of the objectives of my trip to these remote regions of Ethiopia. I had determined that the African civet, like its close Indonesian cousin, did in fact feast on coffee cherries and beans, though it lived a world away from its Kopi Luwak–producing relative.

I was overwhelmed by every imaginable emotion. It was three-thirty in the afternoon and, after more surveying and more collections, I declared the trip a success. I made my way back to the vehicle, having thanked and rewarded my fellow scouts for their assistance, for without them I could not have accomplished this feat. I thanked God for hearing my prayers and answering them by allowing me once again to make an important discovery, one that would permit me to further my study of Kopi Luwak coffee beans. In the comfort of my laboratory I would have the opportunity to peer more deeply at these beans and marvel at their hidden wonders.

The next day we drove to Metu, a town near the Sudanese border. The joy of the previous day quickly turned to fear when a uniformed officer stopped us on the road. He reported that just two hours earlier and a few short kilometres away, eight United Nations workers had been slaughtered as they ran from their vehicles away from rebels who had made their way over the Sudanese border. These rebels were still on the loose, and the officer told us to leave as our lives would certainly be in danger. We were also told that Ethiopian soldiers were on their way to set up a perimeter and secure the area, and that if we remained any longer we would be detained for weeks behind the perimeter. We turned the vehicle around and moved as quickly as we could in the opposite direction. Minutes later we saw military vehicles coming in the opposite direction to set up the perimeter. Fortunately, we had made it out in time.

After my near miss with death at the mouth of a hungry lion just a few days earlier, the last vestiges of my false sense of security in the Land Cruiser disappeared. Had we arrived at this spot just two hours earlier, we could easily have been among the unfortunate victims of the unspeakable slaughter on that very road. The terrorist al Qaeda forces that I had feared so much in my travels in Indonesia had Ethiopian counterparts in a band of nameless thugs who had no respect for the sanctity of human life. An animal—a lion, for example—would kill in order to obtain food to survive, but humans are the only creatures who kill for absolutely no reason.

In Darimu, we managed to phone and reassure our families from a primitive telephone hut that we were safe and well. Incongruously it contained a generator and modern telecommunications equipment. There, we were also able to befriend a farmer who actually raised civets for the musk trade. He agreed to show us the animals, something that had been denied us previously. In a darkened and smoke-filled hut, we saw rows of handmade branch cages. I took a closer look and came face to face with my first African civet.

It was truly an exciting moment! The farmer agreed to let me photograph the hut, the cages, and the animals. In an outside courtyard, he also showed me the centuries-old procedure of collecting musk from the animals with a spoon made from bone. The musk was then placed in a hollow horn, and I was given a sample to analyze. Not for the first time, I wondered at the contrast between the helpful local people and the corrupt bureaucrats.

From Darimu, we made our way to Goliso and then to Gimbi to take further measurements and samples whenever possible. In a flea-infested house in Gimbi, we were told to head northeast towards Nekempte, an area where the African civet was known to live.

That evening we stayed in Bedele. We decided to have dinner in the only place that was open, a very rundown mud-and-dung hut. As I was eating the injera, a common Ethiopian flat bread with lamb and stewed beef, I noticed two cockroaches on the wall in front of me. Having finished my meal, I observed one of them moving downwards. From there it ran across the table and off the end of it. It was large—approximately eight centimetres long. Moments later, the second cockroach followed, but this uninvited guest ran across the table into my dish of remaining food and started to eat it. I yelped in astonishment but the big brown beast remained, feasting on the remnants of my dinner. Everyone in the restaurant looked at me with surprise...cockroaches were a common part of life in this area...nothing unusual. So, why all the fuss?

My room that night was barely large enough for a rickety old single-sized bed. It was built of the same mud, dung, and straw combination of which the other buildings were constructed. The walls, although painted, were very rough. I had to laugh. I had just pulled my new-found coffee beans from the darkness of a dung heap, and now the beans and I were taking shelter in an even larger dung heap! Everything was made of dung here. Instead of having the wall-to-wall broadloom carpeting that adorns most tourist accommodations around the world, here I had wall-to-wall poop.

Several cockroaches spotted the walls and ceiling; this was, literally, a Cockroach Motel. I got into my sleeping bag with my clothes still on. I worried about the coffee beans I had collected—might the cockroaches detect them? I put them in my vest jacket. So there I was, sleeping in a rickety old bed in a dung heap, keeping my precious samples close to my chest to protect them from the oversized ever hungry giant cockroaches. What a night! It reminded me of similar nights I spent fully dressed in the rainforests of Indonesia, but there it was not the cockroaches that were in charge... it was the rats.

The following morning began the long trip to Nekempte where we met a man who trapped civets and sold them to musk producers. He agreed to show us where he collected his civets. At our first location we could see the burrows in which the animal sleeps during the day. Then we went to our second location approximately ten minutes away, and made our way into the bushes, some of which had a bountiful supply of ripe coffee cherries hanging from the branches. The trapper showed us some twigs on the ground spread with small quantities of civet musk. He told us that the African civet is solitary, and marks its territory with musk to warn other civets to stay away from its territory. This also guarantees an ample food supply near the civet's burrow.

About ten metres away, in a slightly sunken area, we saw a collection of civet scats all spread out in a single line. This was a "civetry," a place where the civet usually relieves itself. Like its musk, the civet uses scats to mark its territory. Out came the gloves and camera, and photographs were taken, data and samples collected, and the scats probed with a twig. My investigation revealed not one but approximately forty coffee beans per pile. I was overjoyed and overwhelmed! I was now certain that the evidence of coffee bean ingestion and excretion I had found earlier was not an anomaly, but rather a common trait of the African civet.

I knew I was on to something. But the work had just begun. After more exploration, more sample collecting, and more interviews with locals, my trip came to an end. In Addis Ababa we went out with a bang—literally—when our vehicle was rammed from behind by a city bus. We had travelled thousands of kilometres on either bumpy roads or dry and dusty riverbeds, avoided the moving hazards on the "road," endured the scorching sun, layers of dust, encounters of the wild kind, three clutch repairs, three flat tires, and now we were involved in an undesirable encounter with a mechanical beast. Fortunately, no one was injured either on the bus or in our van. The car escaped undamaged but the bus was not so fortunate…it was totally destroyed.

I was tired and eager to go back home to Canada, but still sad to leave.

On my arrival home, I raced to the laboratory to begin my experiments. I did not even take the time to rest from my journey as I was still working on the adrenaline from my adventures in Ethiopia.

Under the high-powered scanning electron microscope it was evident that the etching characteristics on the beans from the African civet were nearly identical to those on the beans from the Indonesian palm civet, indicating that no apparent difference in processing existed between the two civets. It was like looking at ballistic fingerprints on two bullets and finding that both had been fired from the same gun. But would this similarity lead to identical taste profiles for the two coffees? In order to answer this, I carefully fingerprinted the proteins in both sets of beans. Although protein breakdown (proteolysis) did occur in the coffee from the African civet, the fingerprint pattern was visibly different from that of the coffee from the Indonesian palm civet. At this point I suspected that the flavour profiles would also be different but I wanted to be sure.

Fortunately, since I had performed my initial Kopi Luwak research, a new type of analytical equipment called an electronic nose had become available for use. This machine could detect and measure the aroma profiles of roasted ground civet coffee beans and compare them with those of their corresponding controls. Aroma is a crucial component of taste, a message that is reinforced for us with every illness that plugs our nose and makes our food tasteless.

Interestingly, all the control coffee beans appeared to have similar aromatic profiles, whereas the Kopi Luwak from Indonesia and that from Africa were slightly different from one another. The electronic nose indicated that processing differences between the Indonesian and African civet digestive tracts produce distinct aroma and flavour profiles. These results would be in direct agreement with the differences observed in the proteolytic protein fingerprints, leading to the production of different flavour and colour compounds formed from reactions between the proteins and "sugars" in the beans during high temperature roasting. These substances would, in turn, be partially responsible for the overall differences in the aroma and flavour profiles between the Indonesian and African civet coffees.

I further confirmed these results by "coffee cupping," or having the coffees systematically tasted, smelled, and graded by a certified coffee cupper. The cupper, who did not know the nature of the coffees he was testing, found very little difference in the overall flavour and aromatic attributes between all the control beans. This was in keeping with our electronic nose data. The cupper was able to differentiate the two civet coffees from their controls. This also agreed with the objective electronic nose data. After much deliberation, the cupper was able to find a slight difference between the flavour of the Kopi Luwak from Indonesia and the one from Ethiopia. Since the difference was so slight, Ethiopian Kopi Luwak appeared to be a suitable substitute for the Indonesian version.

This was a very exciting conclusion as it indicated that we had two variants of the same type of coffee. What a find! It was analogous to having two different-tasting wines from the same type of grape, but fermented in two different ways or grown on two different hillsides or fermented with different types or varieties of yeast strains. In fact, it could be said that the passage through the civet's GI tract was very similar to the wine fermentation process. According to several researchers, fermented (wet-processed) coffees have a better overall quality than those prepared by dry processing. In the coffee industry, wet-processed coffees are known to be of superior flavour and as such command a much higher price than their dry-processed counterparts. When the coffee cherries are processed through the digestive tract of either the Indonesian or African civet, they do indeed undergo a type of wet processing due to acidification in the stomach and then fermentation in the intestines due to the natural microflora. Several researchers have found that mucilage degradation seems to be correlated to acidification (similar to what the coffee cherries would experience due to gastric juices in the civet's stomach). Although researchers have found that microbial growth is necessary, it does not directly participate in mucilage degradation by enzyme production but rather limits off-flavour development due to the production of various organic acids. Even more interestingly, research further shows that wet-processing systems work best with lactic acid bacteria, so the system stays as close as possible to a natural neutral fermentation. Lactic acid bacteria are a major colonizing bacteria in the digestive tract of the civet. Given these findings, the unique and characteristic flavour of civet coffee could be due to the unique type of wet processing it undergoes in the civet's GI tract.

Clearly, the type of fermentation is of the highest importance in producing fine flavours. Where we typically drink coffee from cups or mugs, the Indonesians serve Kopi Luwak in a glass like a fine wine. Perhaps the Indonesians are on to something.

With most of my analytical tests completed, the time had now arrived for the ultimate and most crucial test of all. It was time to taste the Indonesian and African Kopi Luwak coffees to determine for myself if I could detect any of the differences described by the independent coffee cupper. Not too surprisingly, I found that both the flavour and the aroma of Kopi Luwak coffee from both Indonesia and Ethiopia were quite distinctive as compared with their non-civet-produced counterparts. In each of the Kopi Luwak coffees I noticed that the top note was that of dark chocolate, with this flavour being notably more pronounced in the Kopi Luwak from Indonesia. On the other hand, the secondary "earthy" and "musty" notes were more pronounced in the Ethiopian coffee. As to acidity, both were basically on par but lower than would be expected for a typical arabica coffee bean.

So which coffee was better: the Kopi Luwak from Indonesia or that from Ethiopia? I leave this decision up to each and every coffee aficionado privileged or brave enough to get their hands on some of each!

MOROCCO

ARGAN OIL, A.K.A. GOURMET GOAT-DUNG OIL

Finding two very similar types of Kopi Luwak coffee produced by two distinct civet species inhabiting countries in different continents was incredible. Never in my life could I have imagined that I would analyze coffee that had been excreted from a catlike creature. Even less likely was the idea that I would trek through the wilds of Indonesia and Ethiopia to find, and study it. But my adventures were only beginning.

A few months after my departmental presentation about Kopi Luwak coffee, Amy, a student who had just returned from a two-month stint studying abroad in Morocco, came down to my lab with a bottle covered in paper and over-wrapped in plastic. She said, "Open it. It's for you." What could it be, I wondered, and quickly saw that it was a container of golden-coloured oil. She asked me if I knew what type of oil it was. I said that I did not, though I thought it smelled faintly like roasted peanuts. She told me that it was argan oil, expressed from argan "nuts" that grow on a tree found in the semi-arid regions of Morocco. (They are not nuts in the true botanical sense.) She then laughed and asked me if I knew how the oil was produced. When I admitted that I did not, Amy told me that argan oil was produced from argan nuts taken from the excrement of a goat. The goats climb the argan trees to eat the nuts, and the herders collect the result. They wash, de-hull, and roast the nuts, and express the oil for use in cooking.

I thought Amy was kidding me as I was sure Kopi Luwak coffee beans were unique among food products in coming out of an animal's back end. Could this be one of those urban myths that propagate and float around until people actually believe them? Having just travelled the world in search of the truth behind the Kopi Luwak legend, I was not so quick to dismiss the story out of hand as I might formerly have done; I had already been proven wrong once. Still, I was skeptical. Civets climbing coffee plants and eating coffee beans is one thing, but huge goats climbing trees and eating nuts is something else altogether! The only tree-climbing, nut-eating animals that came to mind in my part of the world were squirrels. Once, when I was completing my graduate degree at the University of Guelph, one of these had even broken into my office and eaten my peanut butter sandwich but that is as far as things went. I couldn't really imagine goats climbing trees!

But Amy told me she had seen it with her own eyes. She went on to explain that it was one of the rarest and most expensive food oils in the world. Argan oil sold for around 120 American dollars per litre and was used in everything from foods to cosmetics.

Amy went on to recount the whole ordeal she had gone through to bring back this oil to me. At the airport in Morocco, the airport police initially refused to let her take the oil on board the plane. Knowing what type of oil it was, they probably wanted to confiscate it for their own personal use. Amy would not budge, and said she would not leave without it. The police finally allowed her to board the plane but, a few minutes later, some officials arrived and asked her to relinquish the oil. She refused, and they ordered her to leave the plane. When she returned to the inspection area, an argument broke out about the oil, and the inspectors told her that it must remain, saying that Canada would not permit it in the country and it would be best to leave it in Morocco. What these officials did not know about Amy was that she is a level-headed and strong-willed person who would not easily give in. She kept saying that she was taking it back to her professor for research purposes. After a tense half-hour, they finally relented, allowing her to take her half-litre of oil.

After hearing Amy's story, I was indeed intrigued and decided to find out more about this strange, exotic, golden-red oil with such unusual origins. I began searching for information about argan oil and discovered that what Amy was telling me was actually true. I even found a couple of pictures on the Internet showing goats in trees. Not being one to believe everything I see on the Internet, however, I wondered whether these goats had been superimposed onto those trees in some crafty way. After years of working as a food scientist, I had witnessed several episodes of creative tampering with food products in an attempt to get money.

The more deeply I probed into this topic, the more support I found for Amy's description of the origins of argan oil. Even so, I remained skeptical; this could be nothing more than a well-orchestrated hoax. After a few months of exploring the topic, I decided it was time to go one step further and start making some contacts.

I made inquiries about the oil and was referred to an oil exporter by the name of Gilbert. He told me that it was crucial to time my visit to Morocco to coincide with the argan nut season, usually around the middle of July. The indigenous Berber people collected some argan nuts themselves, but the time-honoured method of using goats was still very much alive. Gilbert promised to do what he could to facilitate my trip, but he was a very busy businessman who travelled the world finding buyers for this very rare and special oil. He proved to be knowledgeable about numerous oils with various nutritional and medicinal properties.

I prepared myself as best as I could for the trip to Morocco. On the plane, I jotted down notes about the argan tree and its oil as well as various questions I wanted to ask my host. I also made a list of samples that I would need to collect in order to conduct the type of chemical tests I needed to perform in the laboratory upon my return.

I arrived at the airport in Casablanca, the cultural capital of Morocco, and scrambled to get my things for the long trip into the heart of the city. Remembering the frightening ride in a broken-down taxi through the slums of Addis Ababa in Ethiopia, I had asked my hotel if they could hire a car to come and pick me up at the airport. But my skepticism rose as I saw the hired driver's barely legible sign, and the assortment of spare parts in the trunk of his old white Mercedes-Benz hardly increased my confidence. The seats were hard from use, and the leather was bleached and torn. When the driver started the engine, it shook the whole car like a bowl of jelly, and sounded more like a tank than a sedan. The traffic was unbelievable! I had never seen so many cars so intent on being ahead of each other.

Feeling the heat, I asked the driver to open my window for me. He reached down and pulled off the handle from his window and handed it to me in the back seat. Apparently, there was only one for all four windows! I was utterly shocked! I tried to show that I was okay with this, but stumbled as I tried to find the nut on which to place the handle. After I managed to open my window, he reached back for the handle. Shortly thereafter, the piece of cardboard the driver used as a sun visor got sucked out through the window. I had to wonder how many other parts we were going to lose along the way. The taxi got us where we were going, though—not bad for a car that had been on the road for twenty-four years.

Having made it to the hotel, the taxi driver took my luggage and set it in the middle of the street. I pulled it back quickly before anyone could drive over it. I paid him right away and gave him a tip. The tip, I supposed, was for not getting me killed.

Inside the hotel, I approached the young man at the front desk. I gave him my name and he asked me how I had found the taxi ride. What could I say? I was standing there in one piece…that should say it all! Then I noticed a strange contraption beside the gentleman with all sorts of wires coming from out of it. It turned out to be the hotel's eighty-year-old telephone system! I could have died! It was older than the two of us put together. He said it was in good working order, but I couldn't help recalling the "well-preserved" taxi I had just exited.

Seeing the telephone, I asked him if there was a computer café anywhere around. He got up and escorted me to a cubicle where he showed me a brand new computer that I could use. What a country of contradictions: alongside the ancient vehicles on the street and the antiquated telephone systems sat state-of-the-art electronic equipment. As I looked around, I noticed a small camera installed over the desk. Amused, I thought to myself that they did not want anyone to run off with the antique switchboard.

The young clerk showed me to the cramped turn-of-the-century elevator and proceeded to squeeze my luggage and me into it. My room was on the third floor, and had a beautifully painted door. The room was dark but boasted a small television with three channels, two in Arabic and one in French. I was so tired that I just lay on the bed and immediately fell asleep from sheer exhaustion. I woke up a few hours later and went downstairs to call Gilbert and inform him that I had arrived but, much to my distress, the message on his answering machine indicated that he was in Switzerland on business. I left a message for him to call me at the hotel, telling the clerk that when the call came in I wanted to be awoken right away. Returning to my room, I went back to bed and slept soundly until the next morning.

Having my morning shower, I discovered that this hotel apparently did not possess a hot water heater. At the front desk, I was a bit concerned to learn that Gilbert still had not called me. After my breakfast of the best fresh-squeezed orange juice I had ever tasted, croissants, and buttered toast with peach marmalade, I decided that I would explore the city. The streets of Casablanca are narrow, and cars made their way up and down them with great difficulty. When two vehicles met, one would have to either back up or invade the sidewalk. You took your life into your hands when you crossed the road. There were absolutely no discernible rules. Traffic signals were merely suggestions. I understood this when I saw that many of the lights were so badly positioned that they were impossible to see. I decided to follow the locals' lead when crossing the street; there had to be safety in numbers!

Casablanca was a city that bombards the senses from all sides. Women wearing the chador, or Islamic religious headdress, walked alongside women dressed in typical North American-style clothing. I was impressed by the prevailing attitude of tolerance. The streets were dotted with small cafés filled with people drinking coffee from short glasses. It seemed that all the men smoked. Exploring the stores, I saw many of the different types of food the Moroccans produced and sold. Finally, I entered a store and found what I had been looking for—a 250 millilitre bottle of argan oil. I purchased it for an amount approximately equal to the average Moroccan worker's daily wage.

Happy, I walked back to the hotel to see if Gilbert had called me. As soon as I got there, Mohamed, the front desk clerk, indicated that no one had called. I think he could see how upset and concerned I was getting. I sat down at one of the small tables in the breakfast area to think things over. Shortly thereafter, Mohamed came over and sat with me. He asked why I looked so worried and why it was so important for me to meet this person named Gilbert. I explained to him that I had travelled to Morocco to study argan oil and the unique method of its production, and that Gilbert was my one and only contact in the country.

Mohamed was surprised that I knew about argan oil, and told me that it is very important to people in Morocco. He went on to explain that the oil is produced in the area between Agadir and Essaouira, approximately five hundred kilometres down the coast southwest of Casablanca, in a semi-arid region of Morocco. The Berber people had produced this oil for centuries and had introduced it to the world. Mohamed said that 70 percent of all Moroccans have Berber blood in them but many refuse to acknowledge their ancestry. This was due to a combination of factors, including an overwhelming desire for modernization and a dislike of the Berbers' refusal to adopt Islam.

Mohamed told me that he was proud of his Berber roots and that he had grown up in Agadir, in the heartland of argan oil production. I then asked him if it was true that the goats climbed up into the trees to eat the nuts that get turned into oil. "Of course," he said nonchalantly. To him this was normal. He had grown up seeing goats in trees. He explained that goats like to climb. They began with the lower branches and slowly made their way higher and higher in the tree. He went to the back of the hotel and returned with some argan oil, saying that this was the oil his grandmother produced and sent to him through his uncle. It had a beautiful nutty flavour. Mohamed told me that it was a mixture called Amlou, made with 40 percent orange blossom honey, 40 percent regional almonds, and 20 percent argan oil. It was eaten in the morning with bread, but only by those who could afford it. He volunteered to contact his relatives and tell them that I would be coming so they could show me around their place.

The following day there was still no word from Gilbert. I asked Mohamed if he could help me arrange transportation to the argan area to see the trees and the oil production. He immediately began to make calls, and said that it would probably be better for me to take the train or bus down to Essaouira and Agadir.

I returned to the computer in the booth near the reception area and began checking to see what my students were up to in Canada. It was really amazing to me that I could be teaching a Web-based course and be communicating with my students in Canada, the United States, and as far away as China from a hotel in Northwest Africa. This was a place of contradictions, with twenty-five-year-old taxis roaming the roads and still seemingly older telephone systems dating back to time immemorial coexisting peacefully alongside computers that brought me to the forefront of teaching technology. I was able to read the conferencing messages sent back and forth among the 160 students in one of my courses while simultaneously assigning them their grades with a click of the mouse—all from Morocco. I smiled to see these marvels of technology in a rather unexpected place.

While I was enjoying the recent advances in technology, Gilbert arrived. I was ecstatic! We spent some time chatting in the booth about my arrival in Morocco and the activities with which I had been involved so far. I excitedly told him how I had found some argan oil in a local supermarket, all on my own, and how I was learning about the Moroccan culture and lifestyle. Gilbert informed me that the oil I had purchased was actually produced by his company, and that it was one of the largest argan oil producers in the country. We then went to Gilbert's office for coffee where he explained that he had just arrived from New York, not Switzerland, as his message had indicated.

Gilbert's world-class, argan-oil-packing facility was just five years old, and it was clear that he had invested his life savings in it. Originally from Switzerland, Gilbert became interested in the argan tree and its oil during business trips to Morocco. He told me that after a life-changing event, he had wanted to establish a business that not only made him money to live on but at the same time helped the people who made the product he was selling. He was passionate about this principle, and I could see that he was a sincere man of integrity and goodwill. When we arrived at his house I met his wife and children, and sampled many of the different types of argan oil that he produced. Not all of them were goat processed. He specialized in the nuts that were collected by hand and put through industrial grinders. I even got to taste an argan oil ice cream that Gilbert had commissioned in France, a specialty ice cream used in various food expositions in order to build awareness of argan oil.

The following morning, Gilbert arrived punctually as I stepped out of the hotel, packed and eager to go. We started our trip to the ancient argan groves by going back to his office to get an extra set of bottles in which to collect the various samples of oil during the trip. Gilbert advised that we also pick up bottled water, as the areas we would be visiting were not only hot but extremely dry. This reminded me of the provisions of water we needed to carry with us when we explored the arid regions of the savannah in southern Ethiopia in search of the African civet.

On the way to our first stop, Gilbert explained the importance of the argan tree in the lives of the Berber people. The 8–10 meter tall argan tree (*Argenia spinosa* L.) is a medium-sized, thorny evergreen tree growing primarily in the semi-desert areas of southwestern Morocco, and can live from 150 to 200 years. The tree bears a plum-sized fruit, similar in size and shape to the olive and contains a stone-like structure encapsulating one to three kernels with high oil content. The trees are incredibly adaptable to the harsh, semi-desert climate of southwestern Morocco. Currently, 828,000 ha are under cultivation and this area is now declared a UNESCO Biosphere Reserve due to its uniqueness. When they start to feel the effects of a drought, they shed all their leaves and go dormant. They can remain this way, without leaves, for years. When moisture reappears, they start to bloom again. Argan trees' root systems can reach for water forty metres below the earth's surface. Their leaves are adept at absorbing all available moisture from the air.

Without the tree, human life in the desert would be unable to exist, as the argan supplied all the necessities of life in areas that were inhospitable to other vegetation. It provided food for the goats, which in turn produced milk for cheese and meat for food. The wool of the goats was used for clothing, and the wood from the tree was used to build shelters and as fuel. Argan wood could also be carved and traded for other necessary goods. The nuts that passed through the goat produced precious oil used in the preparation of meals, and the high-protein cake left after oil production was used to feed other livestock. All living things in the desert could also find temporary restful shade under its branches.

The argan tree was so important to the livelihood of the Berber people that they believed it to be sacred. In each location, one tree was left untouched. No fruit was picked from it and no animals were allowed to graze on it, out of respect for the tree that gave the Berbers the means to live. Unfortunately, due to exploitation by individuals who wanted to realize short-term profits from the valuable and sought-after oil, improper tree management practices were causing many trees to die. Some of the pruning procedures led to tree death, resulting in dramatic drops in production. The sacred tree was being desecrated, all in the name of profit.

On the way to the argan fields, we visited an industrial plant that processed argan oil. Gilbert showed me the equipment used to squeeze the precious oil from the seeds. It took one hundred kilograms of fresh fruit or 3,500 fresh nuts to produce thirty-seven kilograms of dried fruit or seventeen kilograms of dried "nuts." These dried fruits and "nuts" in turn contained two and a half kilograms of seeds that finally translated into a litre of oil. The production process was very labour-intensive.

Our next stop was an argan tree nursery that Gilbert had helped to establish. Gilbert recognized the necessity of having a continuous supply of little trees to replace the older ones that were destroyed by fire if he was to continue to produce at acceptable levels. He gave these seedlings to the people to plant next to the larger trees. He also had developed special devices to protect the tender shoots of the seedlings from being eaten by the goats that roamed the argan fields. Gilbert asked if I would like to take one with me to plant in the fields once we arrived. I picked up a seedling and gently placed it in the car. From there we stopped to have a traditional Moroccan lunch of camel meatballs and strips of charcoal-barbecued camel meat. It was delicious, but I found the meat to be tough. Gilbert said that the camel I was eating had been raised solely for food purposes. I don't think he quite knew what to say when I commented that as the meat was a little tough, that particular camel must have seen some mileage.

About 100 kilometres from the argan tree nursery, we saw beautiful mounds of dried sea salt collected from the Mediterranean Sea. The salt came in every imaginable colour. The most beautiful were the salts with high manganese levels that produced a lovely pink hue. As one of Gilbert's projects was to incorporate salt and argan oil for cosmetic facial scrubs, we collected some of the pretty salts. As we were leaving the site, we saw some saltwort plants growing alongside the path. Once turned to seed, this saltwort could also produce a unique and valuable nutritional oil. It struck me then that many of the plants that thrive in inhospitable environments contain life-sustaining products. With a little ingenuity, these treasures are there for the taking.

Four hundred kilometres later, we entered a rocky region. There was not a blade of grass to be seen anywhere! Gilbert pointed his finger into the distance at an argan tree growing right out of the rock. At the top of a large summit, Gilbert stopped the car and told me to get out and look around at the land of the argan. As far as I could see, there were argan trees of every size, shape, and age in this semi-desert environment. I had finally arrived!

Oil production aside, the trees were beautiful in their own right. They reminded me of the bonsai trees I used to grow as a teenager before life became too complicated and my career took over every available moment of my life. The tree trunks and branches were unbelievably gnarled due to the harsh climate and prevailing dry winds that plagued this area of the country. The leaves were tiny, elongated, and succulent, and were similar in size and shape to a sunflower seed. The "nut" containing the oil-rich seed is not a true nut; more correctly, it is the stone inside a type of fruit called a drupe, like olives, peaches, plums, cherries, coffee and mangoes.

We got back in the car and travelled another fifty kilometres, and that was when I saw them—goats in the trees! I jumped out and ran as fast as I could to the trees, but my running towards the goats scared the animals right out of the branches. They jumped out like sailors deserting a sinking ship, and some nearly hit me as they scrambled down. Gilbert laughed at my excitement to see goats in trees. He told me we would see much more of that...he was absolutely correct! We had entered another world.

Again we stopped to see the trees and get a closer look at the terrain. Our water had run out at this point, but we only had a few hours to go before we could stop for the night. We saw a camel skeleton and a group of Berber men collecting argan nuts for making oil. And here was evidence of the validity of another unlikely story: a dung heap from which the nuts had been removed, just as I had been told. I took a photo of the men working.

A man approached and signalled to us to ask if we wanted to drink some tea. Gilbert, not knowing the Berber language, signed that we would accept their hospitality. The man boiled water over an open flame made from dried argan tree branches and then poured the tea into a small glass. We drank it, and the man then signalled an invitation to eat, and brought out oil, honey, and bread for us. I asked Gilbert why they were so kind to us, sharing what little food they had. He said that, in their culture, hospitality meant everything. We were strangers to their land and they wanted us to feel welcome. When I considered that, according to Mohamed, the Moroccans generally did not believe that the Berber people were living according to God's word, I was indignant. In freely and generously feeding the hungry, they were doing exactly that!

Before we went on our way, the argan nut gatherers brought over a jug of water. It was poured into a communal cup and we all took a turn drinking from it. My mind flashed back to the window handle in the taxi. Although there was only one, it served the purpose. The use, not the quantity, is what matters. Drinking from a communal cup also reminded me of my church. Many churches around the world make use of a communal sacramental cup as a symbol of spiritual as well as bodily unity among those who partake. I felt that same sense of unity here. There was something truly spiritual in this act, as we, complete strangers, shared the life-giving water with the inhabitants of this difficult but beautiful country. Now we were no longer strangers, but friends. Giving this gift of hospitality to strangers was a sacred obligation.

We thanked the Berbers for their hospitality. I asked Gilbert if we should give them some money, but he said this would offend them. What could we give them, then? From his knapsack Gilbert pulled out a small bottle of argan oil. This, he said, would make them happy—and it did.

Before we left this semi-desert area, I wanted to collect some argan nuts off the ground and some from the dung piles left behind by the goats. I continued at this task for quite a while, eagerly collecting more and more samples. The ground was incredibly dry and virtually devoid of any type of vegetation except for the large, majestic argan trees. I lost sight of Gilbert but went happily along collecting my samples for testing in the laboratory. For comparison purposes, I also collected some nuts from the tree branches. I could feel the sharp spines of the fruit pricking me like thousands of sharp needles. My forearms became covered in scratches, and I had to agree that the collection of nuts from the trees was something the goats would be better suited to do.

Then I saw another dung pile and decided that, since I still had my gloves on, I would collect a few last nuts before I turned back. As I reached down to start my final collection, something moved on the ground about a foot from my hand. Not knowing what it was, I naturally pulled my hands back right away and took a closer look. It was a gigantic scorpion camouflaged against the dark grey and earth-tone colours of the ground below. My shock was understandable; had I been just a few inches closer, I could easily have been stung! The gloves that protected me from the micro-organisms in the dung would have offered no barrier to the sting of this scorpion. The scorpion would have won, "tails up." Strange, unknown dangers existed in this alien land. My mind went back to Ethiopia and my near escape from becoming a hungry lion's lunch while looking for Kopi Luwak coffee. I felt that I had cheated death once again, all in the name of science and adventure.

For a few moments I just stood still with my heart pounding in my throat and my eyes transfixed on the scorpion. As it scurried away, I marvelled at the frequency of my exotic journeys in pursuit of food legends. Although my laboratory had its own hazards, at least I could control that environment most of the time—not so with these wild, remote places. I wasn't cut out to be a crocodile hunter, and I was certainly no Indiana Jones! I felt more like Mr. Magoo, the oblivious cartoon character who somehow avoids calamity after calamity without even realizing it. I know God was looking after me, but I think even He must be a little worried about me sometimes!

When I got back to Gilbert, I asked him about the scorpion I had seen, and he told me that the argan areas were prime habitats for them. He went on to tell me that many argan nut collectors are stung by scorpions, and that some unfortunate collectors die every year as a result of those stings as medical attention is so far away and the desert shows no mercy to those so wounded. It was a harsh reality. I began to realize that there were inherent natural risks to the collection of the many food delicacies I studied.

That night, we stayed in a small hotel in the city of Essaouira, near the coast. In the morning we made our way to the countryside to visit the areas where the argan nuts were processed into oil. Gilbert explained that traditionally the oil was produced at home, but that now it was made in co-ops by women from the surrounding villages. Each woman could crack up to 3,500 nuts per day, yielding one litre of argan oil. A single tree could only produce a litre at best. Gilbert added that, although these co-ops were run by women, they removed women from their traditional place for making oil in their homes. This had led to a series of problems, especially concerning the education of the women's children.

In the co-op, we saw the entire process. First, the women broke open the "nuts" one by one with a stone.

Then the argan seeds were roasted in a large steel pan held above a wood fire. This gave the argan oil its characteristic nutty flavour. Finally, the women used grindstones to release the oil from the seeds. It is interesting to note that, unknowingly, the women extracting the oil were applying sophisticated scientific techniques to destroy bacteria and release flavour. I postulated that, as with Kopi Luwak coffee beans, I would find much lower bacterial counts than expected for a "food" that had been extracted from feces. This time, however, the difference would be due to roasting, not washing. Ironically, many of the foods I had studied that had passed through an animal's GI tract were much lower in bacteria counts than their controls.

Once again I collected a series of oil and nut samples. I made sure to get samples that had passed through the goat as well as ones that had been produced by modern mechanized ways. Finally, Gilbert took me to a small city called Tamri to meet a man named Mohamed. It was in this town, with Mohamed's help, that Gilbert had begun his work in argan oil. Gilbert recounted that it was very difficult to get started in the trade but that Mohamed had given him a great deal of moral support and taught him much of what Gilbert now knew. Mohamed was extremely kind to both of us, and he treated us to the most lavish lunch in Morocco. We were treated like royalty...we were given everything from roasted chicken dishes to lamb stew, which were luxuries in this poor country. But more than the food itself, the luxury lay in the way the food was offered to us, with and from the heart. It was the same generosity we had experienced while collecting argan nuts in the semi-arid expanse we had just visited. Gilbert explained that hospitality was extremely important in Morocco, and that it was equally important for visitors to receive what was offered...with the heart.

Once the feast was finished, Mohamed's wife brought us many different types of oils from the region to sample. My favourite was the Amlou, the same oil that the other Mohamed had shared with me back at the hotel in Casablanca. It is a rare, delicious delicacy. Then she brought out another honey for me to try—this time, honey from the argan blossom. Among other things, I wondered how they could be sure the bees collected nectar from the argan blossom and not from some other flower. In response to this, she asked me if I had seen any other types of trees or plants growing in this region. She was absolutely right, and I was embarrassed at having asked such a question without thinking, but she was a gracious, patient teacher. On our way out, Mohamed gave me more samples of different types of argan oil to test. He was genuinely generous!

Finally, it was time for us to return to Casablanca. Gilbert needed to catch a plane to Switzerland where he would speak to a major cosmetics firm about the use of argan oil in their products, and I needed to get back to my university lab to start my experimental work. I asked Gilbert to stop the car so I could take one last look at the life-giving argan trees. I wondered if I would ever see these "sacred" trees again. Gilbert advised me to plant some argan trees at the university so I could have them for further study. They are there now nutured with care in the university greenhouses.

Back in the laboratory, I subjected the various argan nuts and oils collected from the different locations in Morocco to a battery of analytical tests. The actual seed that was roasted prior to extracting the oil is composed of approximately 19% protein, 56% lipid, 20% carbohydrate, 2% minerals, and 3% moisture (much like peanuts). Tests quickly revealed that argan oil is of high dietetic as well as culinary value because it contains a high percentage of healthy unsaturated fatty acids, in addition to being rich in aroma and flavour. All the oils I collected were found to contain between 80% and 90% unsaturated fatty acids, 43% of which was oleic acid (a monounsaturated fatty acid), 32% linoleic acid (a polyunsaturated fatty acid), and only a minute amount of linolenic acid (an essential fatty acid belonging to the omega–3 family of lipids).

Linoleic acid (an omega-6 lipid), such as found in argan oil in high quantities (32 percent), is an essential fatty acid that the human body cannot synthesize and must therefore be obtained from dietary sources. Interestingly, diets rich in this fatty acid have been found to prevent rheumatologic and cardiovascular problems. On the other hand, high oleic acid levels have been linked to cardiovascular health, by reducing blood levels of LDL (low density lipo-protein or "bad cholesterol") without affecting HDL (high density lipo-protein or "good cholesterol"). The high levels of both linoleic and oleic acid found in argan oil could be one of the reasons why little cardiovascular disease has been noted in the Berber people who consume this type of oil on a daily basis.

In addition to argan oil's excellent fatty acid composition, it contains over twice the amount of vitamin E as olive oil. A few other important substances such as phytosterols were also found and identified in the argan oil, including spinasterol, schottenol, and stigmasta, with schottenol, a known anti-carcinogen, or cancer-preventing agent, predominating.

Although all the data indicated that argan oil was an extremely healthy oil, what did it actually taste like? Organoleptically (i.e., in terms of the senses), argan oil was found to be very delicate and light in flavour, with a unique aroma. In fact, as a culinary oil, it was comparable to olive oil that is consumed the world over. The deep golden argan oil had a toasted nutty oil aroma with a secondary but pronounced spicy note to it. It is often described as having a "buttery mouth feel" and rich, unique flavour make it important both as a cooking oil and as a flavouring or finishing ingredient. In Morocco, argan oil is usually used on finely chopped tomato salads combined with lemon juice, in richly flavoured tagines (stews), and on couscous as a light finishing drizzle. Combined with honey, yogurt, and fresh fruit, it was a common breakfast dish. It could also be combined with honey and almonds to make amlou, which is famous all over the world.

When I compared argan oil extracted from nuts that had gone through the goat's GI tract to argan oil made from nuts collected by hand (controls), I found many interesting differences. Although the composition of the two oils were nearly identical, they were noticeably different. Most fats in oils are composed of triacylglycerol (TAG) molecules, i.e., a glycerol molecule with three fatty acids bonded to it. The finding of mainly mono- and diglycerides (i.e., glycerol molecules with only one or two fats bonded to it) indicated that the enzyme responsible for digesting fats in the goat's GI tract (i.e., a lipase) had changed the oil by removing one or two fatty acids from the TAG backbone. This is a significant finding to food scientists as this oil's physical and organoleptic properties have been modified by the goats' digestive processes and, as a result, the functionality of this oil has also now been changed. This process would not only produce a perceptible difference in flavour but would also reduce the appropriate cooking temperature. Perhaps this is why the Berber people prefer to use it as a flavour agent rather than a cooking oil. I also studied the melting and crystallization points of the various oils using some very sophisticated pieces of equipment. Argan oil derived from the goat was found to be substantially different from all other oils in the way it melts and crystallizes; it would therefore have a different mouth feel. Interestingly just as with Kopi Luwak coffee beans, as the argan nuts pass through the GI tract, the gastric juices penetrate the nut. But while in Kopi Luwak the main reaction was proteolysis, or protein breakdown, in the argan oil it was inter-esterification, or rearrangement of fatty acids. This rearrangement leads to an oil with different basic properties, which explained the differences in flavour and cooking properties. Despite the fact that the final argan oil produced from nuts that had passed through the goat was very similar nutritionally to argan oil produced from nuts that had not, consumers would immediately be able to distinguish the flavours. I seemed to prefer the oil that had been made from nuts that passed through the goat, but I found an equal split in the number of people who preferred each type.

My trip to Morocco had been a resounding success! I had obtained and tested samples of argan nuts processed through goats and those that had been hand-picked instead. I had seen and experienced Moroccan culture, both in the fabled city of Casablanca and in the countryside. I had learned about and obtained seedlings of the fascinating argan tree. And I had seen goats climbing trees—I would have travelled three times as far to see that! I learned that the prevailing story circulating among food aficionados that *all* argan oil is produced from nuts exiting the backside of the tree-climbing goat is only partially true. Although substantial amounts are produced in this time-tested way, industrialization has now found a way of getting around Mother Nature. In the case of my friend and guide Gilbert, the majority of his argan oil is produced through modern technical means with nary a goat in sight. But I submit that, even in his oil, he does have some of Mother Nature's old ways!

I fully realize that most people would find it strange to voluntarily consume something that had passed through an animal's GI tract and excreted from its anus. Kopi Luwak coffee and argan oil are just two such products. While many might find these foods repulsive and disgusting, however, I dare say most people would not give the matter a second thought if they were unaware of the foods' origins. After all, people don't get squeamish about consuming honey...they even give it to children! I wonder whether most people realize that after the bee ingests the nectar, it goes to the "honey stomach," where it mixes with bodily secretions (enzymes) to get the chemical process started. It is finally regurgitated or "thrown up" in the hive where it continues to be transformed into what we know and enjoy as honey. Yummmmm!

Kopi Luwak coffee and argan oil come out the back end of the animal while honey comes out the front end. So what's the big difference? You tell me!

Dr. Marcone displays his first Kopi Luwak find in Ethiopia. A proud and memorable moment for a food scientist turned explorer on the African continent. On his right is his driver Abebe, and on his left is one of the local guides.

The Land Cruiser used by Dr. Marcone and his guides to travel throughout the remote regions of Ethiopia, serving not only as a means of transportation but also for protection from the wild environment. Note the civet cage as well as spare fuel and water on top of the vehicle.

Dr. Marcone takes another breakdown of the Land Cruiser with good humour in the southern regions of Ethiopia. The vehicle is loaded with extra fuel and water, a necessity on the remote and treacherous roads of Ethiopia as there are no gas stations just around the corner.

Burlap sacks filled with coffee beans ready for export at the Coffee and Tea Authority in Addis Ababa, Ethiopia. Ethiopia is considered to be the birthplace of coffee and also produces some of the finest coffees in the world. This Ethiopian coffee will end up in some of the world's most famous blends.

At the Coffee and Tea Authority in Addis Ababa, Ethiopia, Dr. Marcone cups various Ethiopian coffees under the guidance and watchful eye of the quality control manager. Coffee cupping such as this is performed by trained and experienced coffee "cuppers" or "tasters" with superb taste and smell abilities, and is performed worldwide as the standard method of determining coffee quality much like good wine is evaluated.

The typical savannah landscape with its characteristic acacia trees spread throughout southern Ethiopia. This was a common scene during Dr. Marcone's travels in search for the African civet. Note the flat, dry land typical of this region.

A typical southern Ethiopian hut made from cattle dung with an intricately thatched roof made form locally collected vegetation. The round shape of the hut and the cone shaped roof are characteristic of these huts. Dr. Marcone's accommodations were much the same.

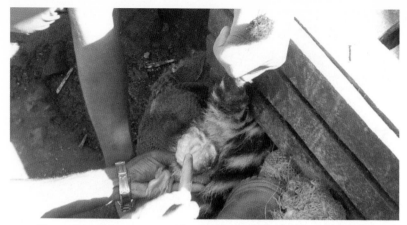

The traditional but controversial method of collecting the musk from the anal glands of the African civet. An indirect reference to musk in Ethiopia dates back to at least the times of the Queen of Sheba who presented gifts of fragrant oils to King Solomon of Israel (1 Kings 10:1–13). Up until recently, musk (a.k.a. civetone) was used as a fixative by the perfume industry. Now an artificial musk is used by many makers of perfume. What an image… anal secretions deliberately put on one's body to enhance the longevity of desirable odour on the body!

Curious children looking into the Land Cruiser wondering who the visitors to their remote village are and their purpose. Dr. Marcone feels like one of the initial explorers of Africa. This may be the first time these children have seen people with "white" skin. The villagers are that remote and isolated.

The collection of a Kopi Luwak coffee scat from the rainforest floor on the island of Sumatra, Indonesia as filmed by two German documentary journalists. One scat was found to contain approximately 200 coffee beans, enough to brew three cups of coffee.

Dr. Marcone discovers his first Kopi Luwak scat on the rainforest floor on the island of Sumatra in Indonesia. This was one of the first indications that Kopi Luwak coffee was not an urban legend as many coffee aficionados had thought.

Dr. Marcone holding a freshly collected Kopi Luwak scat. The leaves were sewn together with grass or veins taken from leaves to form the cup-shaped container.

A close-up of a freshly laid civet scat discovered by Dr. Marcone. Note the shape of the scat, which is typical for the civet and also the great number of coffee beans. The civet uses the scats to mark its territory against other civets, males and females.

Dr. Marcone finally encounters a very young luwak (a.k.a. civet) responsible for producing the Kopi Luwak coffee on the island of Java, Indonesia. They exchange curious glares at one another, full of awe, wonder, and amazement.

On the island of Java, Indonesia, Dr. Marcone is shown grinding Kopi Luwak coffee the traditional way under the careful and watchful eye of an indigenous Javanese woman. While Dr. Marcone was hard at work, she explained the history, origins, and importance of the coffee to her culture.

A feral goat high up in the branches of an Argan tree eating the fleshy fruit containing the oil rich "nuts" from among the long and sharp thorns. The goats are not harmed by stripping the Argan fruit from among the thorns. Note the tiny succulent leaves among the thorns, which are typical of trees in hot and dry semi-desert areas of the world.

Traditionally clothed Berber men collecting Argan fruit fallen to the ground and Argan "nuts" from the goat scats in the semi-arid regions of Morocco. Hospitality, especially to strangers, is a strong religious tradition for the Berber people living in this harsh environment.

Argan "nuts" in baskets displaying various stages of processing. From right to left: first basket contains argan nuts with dried fleshly material still attached; second basket: nuts with the fleshy material removed; third basket: the seed from the cracked nuts; the last two baskets contain various waste materials from the processed nuts.

The first step in argan oil processing. A typical Moroccan woman of Berber descent cracking argan "nuts" to extract the seed containing the oil. She is able to crack 3,600 nuts per day producing approximately 1 liter of the precious golden-red oil. She works in a co-op with other Berber women, which is owned, and operated, by the local women.

MALAYSIA, INDONESIA, AND HONG KONG

"THE CAVIAR OF THE EAST": EDIBLE BIRD'S NESTS, A.K.A. SALIVA SOUP

Soon after my return from Morocco, I leaned back in my chair and pondered the argan oil and the Kopi Luwak coffee obtained from my recent globe trotting adventures. It was not the foods that intrigued me so much as their bizarre processing methods. Prior to my introduction to these foods, I had never imagined that anything excreted from an animal could be considered food, let alone that I would be spending my time studying it. In my travels over the years, I had eaten and drunk many unusual foods and seen non-Western processing methods, but this civet coffee and goat argan oil beat them all! I thought these might go down in history as the most unusual foods ever. But soon I realized that my Western and scientific prejudices were hampering me in my research. Recognizing and setting aside my personal biases opened up entirely new worlds of cuisine.

One day I was shopping in Toronto's Chinatown with a Chinese graduate student when I observed something strange in a window. My curiosity aroused, we entered the store to examine the delicate cup-shaped items enclosed in a glass case, much like jewellery on display. There were white and red "jewels," with the least expensive being the white and the most expensive being the red. The prices ranged from one to ten thousand Canadian dollars per kilogram and, with prices like these, this was probably the most appropriate way to display them.

I stared in silence until the student asked me if I knew what it was. When I replied that I did not, he told me that it was called bird's nest and that, yes, it was edible. I thought it a strange sort of name for the food because I could not see anything that resembled twigs, sticks, or leaves. The store clerk, overhearing our exchange, approached us with a big smile. I asked him about the composition of the nest as it looked very crystalline. The clerk told me that the nest was actually bird saliva. "Bird saliva? You mean it's made of bird *hork*?" I laughed nervously, not wanting to insult the clerk or my friend. Surprisingly, the clerk exclaimed, "Bird hork. You got it!" I did not know what to think! The student turned to the clerk and, with some amusement, told him that I studied foods that were excreted from the back end of animals. The quick-thinking clerk replied that all we had to do was turn the animal around, and then the back end became the front end, so the professor could study this too!

When I returned to my office, I began an in-depth study of these highly desirable and valuable nests. "Bird's nest," I learned, referred to the nests produced by several different swiftlet species in Southeast Asia. Often referred to as the "Caviar of the East," bird's nest is usually cooked with sugar in a double boiler producing a gastronomic delicacy often known as "bird's nest soup." Human consumption of these nests has been a symbol of wealth, power, and prestige for eons; in fact, it was referred to by some as the "Emperor's Food." Its use in traditional Chinese medicine has been documented as far back as the Tang (AD 618–907) and Sung (AD 960–1279) dynasties. Given the close historical ties between food and medicine even in cultures other than the Chinese, I should not have been surprised at its medical use. Hippocrates, one of the greatest Greek philosophers and the person considered to be the father of modern medicine, wrote in 400 BC, "Let food be your medicine." We in the West have strayed from this path but are now coming back to it. The trend is most evident in the development of a number of fortified foods such as flour and milk, nutraceuticals, and functional foods.

I discovered that there are more than twenty-four species of insectivorous, echo-locating swiftlets distributed around the world, but only a few produce edible nests. Most of these come from two heavily exploited species: the white-nest swiftlet (*Aerodramus fuciphagus, L.*) and the black-nest swiftlet (*Aerodramus maximus, L.*), whose habitats range from the Nicobar Islands in the Indian Ocean to sea caves in the coastal regions of Thailand, Vietnam, Indonesia, Borneo, and the Palawan Islands in the Philippines.

The nests are built almost exclusively by the tiny fifteen to twenty gram male swiftlet over a period of approximately thirty-five days. The building material is composed almost entirely of a glutinous substance found in saliva secreted from the swiftlet's two sublingual salivary glands. The hemispherical, self-supporting nests weigh as much as twice the swiftlet's body weight and are usually attached to the vertical concave-face walls of inland or seaside caves. Harvesting the edible nests for human consumption is a painstaking and often dangerous operation for local collectors. Most nests are built hundreds of feet up the walls of dark caves. Harvesting them requires the use of temporary scaffolding made of locally obtained bamboo or ironwood. Unfortunately, unscrupulous collectors often take the nests before the young birds have fledged thereby threatening the survival of the species. This, coupled with increasing demand, puts immense pressure on these two swiftlet species.

After collection, the nests are cleaned. This tedious cleaning process requires almost one hour per nest. It starts with soaking the nests in water until the nest "cement" is softened and the tightly bound strands are partially loosened. Small feathers and fine plumage are manually removed with tweezers, and the cleaned strands are subsequently rearranged and remoulded into chips of various shapes. They are then air-dried and packaged for sale around the world, with the vast majority being sent to Hong Kong. North America, the next largest market, is a distant second. World trade figures conservatively estimate that seventeen to twenty million nests are harvested annually, with the total weight estimated at approximately two metric tons. These "discoveries" piqued my curiosity, and I began to plan a trip to Southeast Asia to separate bird's nest fact from bird's nest fiction.

My long journey began at Pearson International Airport in Toronto. The westward flight took me to Vancouver and then across the Pacific Ocean to Taiwan. After thirty-two hours, I finally landed in Kuala Lumpur, Malaysia. I surveyed the crowd nervously, looking for my host, and finally spotted a person holding up a piece of paper with the words "Prof. Marcone." I breathed a sigh of relief, introduced myself, and we headed to the hotel. Unfortunately, the brief city tour my host granted me has, to date, been my only one.

The next morning we boarded an hour-long flight eastward to Borneo. This beautiful island, shrouded in mystery and intrigue, was to be my home for the next few days. My second host met us, and I felt like the Olympic torch being passed from one runner to another. As I took in the lush green beauty of the surrounding land, my host filled me in on the details of our itinerary. He became my teacher, my mentor, my colleague, and, at times, my guardian. He told me that the edible bird's-nest trade was secretive and dangerous. Natural perils aside, the gangsters who ran the trade did so ruthlessly. My host instructed me not to take any photos or notes unless I asked permission first. Although I was excited about my new adventure, I also became apprehensive.

We made our way to Niah National Park in the heartland of Malaysia's bird's nest trade. We crossed a crocodile-infested river in a very old boat that rocked heavily from side to side. I hoped that I had not escaped being snacked on by an Ethiopian lion and nearly stung by a Moroccan scorpion only to become crocodile food instead. My observant host noticed my uneasiness and inquired if I had seen crocodiles before. In fact I had, I replied nervously, as they were a common sight during my travels in Ethiopia. We had even crossed a river on whose shores many crocs were sunbathing, but then, at least, we had had a revolver for protection. My host laughed heartily and said that I was not accustomed to seeing them. Certainly, I was much more accustomed to seeing them at the zoo than in "real" life. My journey into the murky world of the bird's nest had begun.

After landing safely on the other side, we started the four-kilometre hike through the lush tropical rainforest. Our new guide instructed us not to touch any insect, creature, or plant without first asking, as many could inflict extreme pain and sickness, as they were poisonous even to the point of lethality! Beauty was indeed deceiving, as is often the case in nature. The guide warned that proper medical attention would be extremely difficult to obtain. The point was clearly received and understood.

In light of these unfamiliar surroundings, I walked right behind the guide with my flashlight strapped tightly around my neck. This was the only way I would be able to see what I had come to find in the darkened caverns, and I had not come all this way for my light to slip out of my hands and disappear in the swampy pools. I stopped several times to survey the terrain and the first-growth rainforest trees. As we journeyed deeper, my senses opened to the beauty of my surroundings. I could hear monkeys and birds, and could smell the green plants and other delightful odours emanating from the forest. The large tree trunks dwarfed me in the occasional picture we took in this surreal place.

At last, the caves appeared. Every step brought us closer, and I wondered whether I, as a city dweller and laboratory researcher, would be able to meet the challenges ahead. Hiking became treacherous as the underbrush grew thicker and the ground beneath our feet became more slippery. I was worried about falling into the swampy, parasite-infested pools and rivers that surrounded us. I had plenty of blood but had no intention of sharing it! Though the cave entrances loomed in the distance, my immediate attention was consumed by my efforts to stay upright and intact.

We finally arrived at the first cave and, upon entering, found the remains of a long-gone society. The people had made their home at the mouth of the cave in order to collect the precious nests. I could see how they had cooked, collected water, and slept in these surroundings. We walked around, examining abandoned stone implements and long bamboo nest-collection poles.

In a second cave, we found an archaeological dig started by the Malaysian government a few years before. Unfortunately, it looked abandoned except for the makeshift fencing erected around the site to protect it from vandalism. The host made a rare exception and took me into the site to visit the remains of the original swiftlet nest collectors and traders. There was an air of sanctity about the old burial ground, and I said a small prayer for the ancient collectors. My guide went into a small hut and presented me with an aged, hand-crafted metal nest-harvesting tool. It is a twenty-five centimetre piece of flattened metal with a semi-circular cutting edge at the very top, and it would be lashed to a pole so as to extend the reach of the harvester. This blade is very durable and sharp, and is easily re-sharpened when needed. I was honoured! It felt as though the ancient collectors had passed their trade tool to me, a new explorer, and it was nice to have their blessing. As we journeyed into the cave, I held the ancient tool like a torch in one hand, while in the other I held my modern instruments. It seemed a fitting meld of old and new.

We entered the main cavern, and I saw ironwood poles hanging vertically over seventy-five metres from the top of the cave being "bolted" and lashed together, alternating between the right and left sides of the subsequent pole creating a "straight" line. I was told that the collectors would climb these poles with no safety devices to protect them from a certain and instantaneous death should they fall. The long harvesting tools gave them the ability to reach much further than the area just around them. This saved them the necessity of climbing down and then up another pole within a short distance of the previous one. Climbing was hard work in these dark and humid caves. I looked at the tool in my hand and was awestruck at all that I saw. We made our way deeper into the blackness, surveying what was around us. The rock was rough and varied, and I noted that it had different compositions; some of the rock was pure limestone whereas elsewhere there were other minerals mixed in.

Finally, in a part of the cave so black that the light from our torches seemed an unnatural intrusion, we found them. On the cave ceiling, impossibly high above us, were hundreds of swiftlets in their precious nests. They were dark, to match their environment, and used their echo-locating skill just like bats to fly in total darkness with near-miraculous ease. It was truly amazing!

While I made careful, detailed notes, some of my helpers collected some abandoned nests for me to examine when I returned to my comfortable laboratory. The people helping us were actual nest collectors who had worked in these very caves. They were small in stature, but very fit and strong. They needed their strength and agility to scale the ironwood poles to scrape the nests from the sides of the cave walls. The collectors were instructed to remove the nests with a piece of the rock base plate attached so that this could be examined and tested too. It was a blessing for us that on the third try we got our very first red "blood" nest— the most prized and expensive of all. My initial observation was that the base plate rock of the red nest was much darker than that of the white nests.

As I was examining the nest, something struck me on the shoulder. Believing that it was a nest, I aimed my torchlight towards it, hoping that it had not disintegrated. To my surprise, the nest was completely intact. As I examined it, one of the collectors reached over, grabbed it, and began to squeeze it gently...it was highly flexible. At that point my guide told me that the humidity in the cave ranged anywhere from 70 to 85 percent, which softened the nests. The nests' flexibility allows the baby birds to move around in it without causing it to break or crumble.

We walked for another hour and a half before seeing light again. My guide turned to me with a smile and commented that my collected nests would keep me very busy. If I wanted, however, we could obtain other nests from a different location. He said that there was another remote site noted for its bird's nests and that it might be worth our while to make the trip. The site he was referring to was in Mulu National Park. I agreed that this would be an excellent idea, as it was in my interest to increase the number and variety of nests that I took back to Canada. My guide mentioned that there were only two ways to reach the caves in Mulu as there were no roads leading there. The first was a treacherous journey by boat, but as many people had lost their lives to the unforgiving seas, we opted for the second method—a charter flight straight there. It struck me that the swiftlets lived in a very harsh environment indeed. The physical danger involved in harvesting the nests more than earned the high prestige and price they commanded.

Our small plane made the ninety-minute flight to Mulu and landed at the local airport. Due to the size of the plane, we were only able to take essentials with us. In my case, this included my hiking gear, torch lamp, collection containers and bags as well as experimental materials. We took a small bus to our unusual lodging—it was nine metres above the forest floor! The sleeping quarters and the eating and recreation facilities were interconnected by a series of suspended boardwalks that kept us off the ground. To me it appeared that we were living in a tree house, or in a complex of interconnected rooms built in the clouds. Never in my life had I seen such a large number of integrated shelters hung among trees. They looked very much like the fancy treetop hunting blinds I had seen in many places in Canada and the United States. The only difference was the sheer number of them and how well connected they were. In some places a tree trunk would come right up through the floorboards in the walkway between one shelter and the next.

I spent many hours peering out, listening to the complex songs of crickets and the serenades of birds roosting in the trees. Our high vantage point gave us a bird's-eye view over what seemed like all of God's creation, and it was stunning! Life was different up here. We were captivated by the unnoticed beauty of the sunrise and sunset, the birds, and the animals. We felt the cool breezes just below the tree canopies, providing welcome relief from the oppressive heat. I felt that I could have spent the rest of my life in that lofty sanctuary. A comforting sense of peace and safety infused me, and I finally understood why so many animals make their homes high up in trees.

The next day, we began our journey by boat, along a winding, crocodile-infested river. Once more the riverbanks were lush and green, and an orchestra of crickets, wild animals, the wind in the trees, and the water in the river produced a constant symphony. My memory of this incredible music remains strong and vivid. Upon discovering a hidden village along the bank, we stopped for a visit. I was astonished and more than a bit apprehensive to learn that these people belonged to a tribe of local headhunters. Although they no longer practised the tradition of their forefathers (or so they said), I was informed that many of the heads collected by their ancestors could still be seen in the various compartments of the ancient longhouse.

When I saw the kindness with which we were treated, I realized that I was not in any danger. I noticed a small Baptist church, and was intrigued by the merging of these two very different cultures. Even so, I admit that the idea of headhunters made me jumpy. When a young man asked me if I wanted to see some of the heads his ancestors had collected in their various tribal wars, I felt it was time to go. My guide rescued me, telling the young man that I had to meet another guide at the caves two kilometres away, and we had to be on our way. Relieved, I bid the young man goodbye and walked with my guide to the boat. Once we were on the boat and had pushed away from the shore, I thanked him. I laughed and said that I did not want to lose my head over this encounter. I found it extremely funny that I had worried about losing my head to a hungry lion, and now I was hobnobbing with headhunters. In my business, the head and its contents are the most important parts of the body, and they were not something I could do without! We made our way up the river, being careful to avoid the dead tree branches that had fallen into the river. They seemed innocent enough but could easily harbour crocodiles, waiting for an easy meal of human flesh.

The second time we landed, it was to continue our journey through the rainforest on foot. When we reached the caves, I saw that they were different both from the caves in Niah and also from each other. Some were composed of a type of sandstone, while others had many stalactites hanging from the roof. Swiftlets nestled in the dark ceiling crevices of caves of all types, but I noticed that in these varied caves there was a wider variety of swiftlet species. In addition to the swiftlets that produced white and red blood nests, we saw those that produced a black nest living throughout the cave. Others incorporated moss with their saliva to complete their nests. These nests, although not as valuable, were still gathered by local collectors and processed for the edible bird's-nest trade.

We made our way deeper and deeper into the dark cave until we reached a large inner cavern. It was at least 120 metres tall, and we could hear a large number of bats making their characteristic clicking sounds high above. The noise was loud, as this particular cavern was known to house over one million bats, but it was difficult to imagine such a large number of animals in such a relatively small space. Their clicks, chirps, and chittering sounds filled the air with a sense of motion. We moved to one side and in unison focused our torchlights on the ceiling above. It was almost completely covered in bats! These creatures roost in trees and caves to protect themselves against predators, and only come out in the evening when their predators lose their advantage and must sit on the sidelines. Additionally, the cave ceilings here were a very warm thirty degrees Celsius, unlike the cool floor just below them, which made it a perfect spot for bats to rest and raise their young.

My superstitions and general uneasiness regarding bats got the best of me, and I nervously asked if we could move on. The guide turned to me as I started to walk away and asked what was wrong. I just kept moving without saying a word, while placing a T-shirt over my nose and mouth to guard against the unimaginable stench of closely packed animals and droppings (guano) in the warm, moist cave. Once again the guide approached and asked what was wrong. I said that there were certain diseases that could be transmitted from bats to humans, and that we should not have come into the cave without the proper safety equipment. While researching the area in preparation for this trip in my comfortable lab, I had learned that bats can become infected with a fungus called *Histoplasmosis capsulatum*, which can be excreted through their droppings. The fungus then grows in the nitrogen-rich fertilizer of bat (and also bird) guano, producing fruiting bodies called spores. Inhalation of these spores causes a fungal infection in the lungs which can produce pneumonia-like symptoms in unsuspecting souls. I was certainly not willing to host such an organism; nor was I at all tempted to take such an unpleasant souvenir home with me. To make matters worse, the caves actually increased both our exposure and our risk, as the spores were concentrated there due to the lack of adequate ventilation and wind movement.

The guide turned to me, put his hand on my shoulder, and attempted to reassure me by saying that the bird's-nest collectors came there all the time and were never harmed by the diseases I was worried about. I was not convinced, especially in light of my knowledge that local residents usually developed a natural immunity to those sorts of diseases, but

I decided to keep my mouth shut, the T-shirt over my mouth and nose, and my feet moving swiftly forward. I wanted to leave the place for many different reasons, and standing there talking with the guide wasn't helping.

In the deepest part of the cave, we found a large fresh-water lake. Our guide told us that the natives believed this was the fountain of youth and would often bathe in its waters. One by one we approached the water's edge to flush our faces with this water while the person behind us grabbed the back of our clothes so that we would not fall into the deep darkness of the lake, and disappear under the clear waters. Could this indeed be the fountain of youth that the explorers of old had sought so desperately? In the darkness we could not see our reflections in the water, so we had to wait until we got back into the sunlight to learn if we had indeed been changed by the lake. As my colleagues didn't bat an eyelash at me when we came out, I can only conclude that no dramatic loss of years had taken place.

On our way out of the cave, we collected nests, docu-menting every detail, and taking literally hundreds of photos and copious notes. As we exited the cave at approx-imately six thirty in the evening, the blue skies had started to darken with the setting sun. Dusk was falling and night was at the doorstep...it was imminent. The guide asked me to stop and drink some water to rehydrate, a necessary pre-caution in a tropical climate but one that often escaped my mind. He told me to sit on a large rock, for soon there would be a spectacular natural show in the sky.

I waited and watched as the sky darkened—but not because of the setting sun. Thousands upon thousands of bats emerging from the cave blackened the sky, and for a full ten minutes the exodus didn't stop, not even for one moment. Their high-pitched echo-locating chirps and clicks grew louder and louder, increasing in intensity as more and more bats emerged. They were leaving the cave as a large flock in search of their usual food, insects in the rainforest. Around 7 p.m. the sun disappeared, and darkness crept over us even faster than before. The bats made a long, black, silken ribbon that appeared over the horizon from the cave below and danced in the sky at the whim of the wind. The guide drew closer and told me to watch the bats do their nightly dance in the sky. In unison, the bats formed a circle in mid-air above the cave and made three complete turns in the air. Then, as fast as they had appeared, they disappeared into the rainforest. The dance had ended, the feasting had begun. I had never seen so many bats before, and this eerie experience remained fresh in my mind for a long time.

We left Mulu a few days later and flew back to Miri to meet two bird's nest traders who told me about the dangers of their work. Typically, traders would arrange meetings with collectors at out-of-the-way locations during the night to purchase fifty kilograms of nests. A quick inspection sufficed for an exchange of one hundred thousand American dollars, all in cash! Business was done quietly and in total darkness, and, under these circumstances, murders would occasionally occur. Of course, the traders feared for their lives sometimes, but this was the path they had chosen in life, and they were prepared for the risks. It is much the same with other kinds of traders: they accepted the dangers and enjoyed the benefits.

From Miri, we travelled approximately one thousand kilometres by car, visiting various cities involved in the edible bird's-nest trade. After a long journey we finally arrived at one of the southernmost cities in the Malaysian part of Borneo, Kuching, where 80 percent of the collected nests are processed for international sale. I thought it was ironic that the name of the city means "cat" and that it should be here where the bird's nests are collected and processed. I could imagine a cat's paw metaphorically clawing in the harvested nests.

In Kuching I was given a very special opportunity that few people, Westerners and scientists in particular, have ever been granted: I was allowed to observe the process by which the nests are transformed from regular bird's nests into products suitable for sale. The process is shrouded in secrecy, and even people in the trade know little about this important step. Secretly, I was brought to an undisclosed location surrounded by a huge perimeter wall. Guard dogs lunged at us but were restrained by their handlers. We were given the go-ahead to enter the main building, and it was here that we observed the entire process (with one exception, which will be discussed later).

I was surprised that they permitted me to photograph and videotape the process. I took many notes and documented the chemicals they used: hydrogen peroxide to bleach the nests and remove the feathers, hydrosulfite to clean the nests further, and potash and alum to change the stickiness of the cleaned strands so the nests could be reformed into their final shape. As a chemist, the use of hydrogen peroxide in the process was very interesting to me. Not only would it bleach and clean the nests, but it would also destroy the bacteria associated with them—a good thing, as one can only imagine what is actually on the nests, unseen and unnoticed. I wondered how these seemingly "uneducated" people knew which chemicals to use to prepare the nests for sale. What I saw was a highly guarded and secretive process that few people had ever seen, especially a Westerner like myself. I felt privileged to be allowed to witness the process, but even more privileged to be able to take photographs of the various activities and stages involved in the preparation of edible bird's nests.

We observed the women meticulously cleaning the nests, using tweezers to remove dirt, feathers, broken eggshells, and other undesirable objects. This tedious process took hours. Finally, the cleaned strands would be recomposed into shapes that resembled the original nests. The wet nests were moved to a drying room equipped with a series of light bulbs, fans, and other contraptions to dry them. This room looked much like one of those marijuana-growing operations one sees on a television newscast when the police raid a pot house.

What a privilege it was to see what few others had ever witnessed. I was given the unprecedented honour of tasting every conceivable type of edible bird's nest soup prepared from every type of commercially available nest. In each case, the nest was prepared in the most traditional way, with rock sugar. The cleansed bird's nest would be placed in a small earthenware container and gently simmered, extra water or chicken broth being added as needed due to evaporation. It was cooked until the nest became translucent and soft, which generally took approximately ninety minutes. The cooking time varied due to the thickness of the strands. In the last few minutes of simmering, the rock sugar was added to sweeten the soup, in amounts that were based on personal taste preferences.

Although there were minute differences in flavour, they all tasted very similar to me. The strands in the soup tasted much like the "beads" in tapioca pudding, with the same chewy texture. The nest took on the flavour of the rock sugar and therefore seemed more of a dessert than a typical Western-style soup. This being said, the nests could be prepared in many different ways and take on many different flavours; another popular method was to cook them in chicken broth.

The production manager agreed that there wasn't much difference in taste, but said that people were still willing to pay ten thousand American dollars per kilogram for the red "blood" nests. He told me that people believed the red blood nest was the last nest the bird would build in its life, and that it therefore put its blood into its making and then perished. I replied that I found this hard to believe, especially in light of what I had observed, but that I would have the opportunity to test it in my laboratory.

The one thing that had been hidden from me by the processors was how the nests were adulterated. It seemed that the extra incentive of money far out weighed the danger of being caught giving away "state" secrets. We had previously been informed by the workers that, in an effort to increase the net weight of the nests prior to sale, karaya gum, *Tremella* fungus, and red seaweed were consistently used as adulterants. These materials were incorporated during the processing stages at levels of up to approximately 10 percent of overall weight, and were extremely difficult to detect because their colour, appearance, taste, and texture were so similar to the actual salivary nest cement. Karaya gum is a dried exudation of the stem and branches of *Sterculia urens* (a member of the cacao family), and is insoluble in water. It absorbs water, forming viscous, adhesive strands similar to the nest cement. The white jelly fungus *Tremella fuciformis* is introduced in the form of thin slivers and looks very much like the laminae strands of the bird's nest. Perhaps the most frequently used adulterant is a carrageenan-bearing red seaweed such as *Kappaphycus alvarezii* which, when cut into slivers and boiled, is very difficult to detect in the final product.

That evening, my guide invited one of the workers in the plant to come to the hotel and bring some nests that had been adulterated. I asked her to show us exactly how the adulteration was done so that I could get a first-hand look at the craftiness of these processors. The worker began by painstakingly weaving various adulterants into a nest. She then used a variety of liquids to cement the material of the nest. The final product was so indistinguishable from an unadulterated nest that I had to be careful not to mix them up. I collected a few of these adulterated nests, as they too were important for my research. It was both exciting and disturbing to witness the adulteration of the nests right before my eyes. On the one hand, I was able to see and learn exactly what was used as an adulterant, how the adulterant was prepared before incorporation, and how it was added to blend in with the rest of the nest. This knowledge was of invaluable assistance in my work and would help me to devise ways to detect this type of fraudulent activity. On the other hand, however, I was chagrined to see how easy it was to adulterate the nests, and how nonchalantly the fraudulent activity occurred. I had spent part of my career developing analytical methods to identify the presence and level of adulteration in foods; and I knew that, although I had learned some of their deceitful activities, the fraudsters would always be one step ahead of me in their quest to obtain money illegally.

That night, as I lay in bed, part of me felt very uneasy as though witnessing the evening's activities had somehow contaminated me. I reassured and comforted myself by deciding to use this information to make the adulterators' work that much more difficult.

From Kuching, I flew back to Kuala Lumpur to start the second leg of my journey. In one of the cities that bordered the capital, our guide pointed to a window in a nearby building, saying, "Can you see it, can you see it?" At first I did not understand him, but he explained that the ordinary-looking building contained an artificial environment for swiftlets. I wanted to take pictures, but the guide indicated that that would be too dangerous, as the swiftlet aviary owner had spotted us. We went to another building, ostensibly another artificial swiftlet habitat. This one had cars parked outside and passers-by conducting business in the shops below. This time my guide allowed me to take pictures, but only if I shot from the cover of our vehicle. As in my travels in Ethiopia, Indonesia, and Morocco, the vehicle was my shelter. Many times my guide told me to lower my camera until the coast was clear. When it appeared that someone had seen what we were doing and began to move towards us, my guide started the vehicle, put the pedal to the metal, and drove away as fast as the car could go. He said that he would take me to a location where he himself had helped a commercial landowner set up his own birdhouse within the city limits.

Upon arrival, he left the vehicle and indicated that I should remain behind. He walked into the shop and re-emerged within a few minutes with another man. They came to the car and told me that we would be allowed to enter one of his birdhouses. The shopkeeper then departed and we made our way down some narrow streets. At one point my host told me to look up and, to my surprise, I saw hundreds of swiftlets darting up and down the streets. My host said that the swiftlets enjoyed their life in the city as the narrow streets provided a similar environment to the narrow ridges commonly found outside their caves in the mountains. The abundance of man-made garbage produced an abundance of insects that provided an excellent food source. Indeed, the city did seem like an ideal location for the swiftlets: they had shelter, safety, plenty of food, and an environment that approximated to their natural mountain habitat. At the same time, their coexistence with humans would help to reduce the number of insects within the city limits. Even so, my guide told me that some people objected to these birds, complaining about their droppings on the pavement, sidewalks, and cars. I surveyed the area but did not see many droppings on any object or surface, and commented on this to my host. He informed me that it was just an excuse people used to push for city regulations or ordinances that would force potential operators to move out of the city.

I asked how much one could expect to make from such an operation. Apparently, a small, well-constructed birdhouse of approximately twenty-eight square metres could produce a monthly income of roughly ten thousand dollars. That was a lot of money in Malaysia! This type of business would not only be good for the investor but would permit the investor to collect the nests without endangering himself by climbing sheer cave walls. More importantly, however, it would protect the young hatchlings since the collector could easily see which nests were empty and which were still in use. Here was a wonderful, symbiotic coexistence.

Many floors up and behind numerous steel doors, we found the birdhouse itself. I was quickly overcome by the loud chirping. Momentarily, I feared that the birds would attack me, Hitchcock-style, but my host told me that over half of the chirps we heard were audio recordings to attract new birds to this location. I noticed the Murundi wood on the walls, which was used by the birds to place their nests in the etched grooves; much like the rough rock surfaces in the caves we had visited. I took pictures and samples, and we soon made our way out of the building.

I asked my host the reason for a fountain inside the bird-house. He replied that the water sounds attracted the birds, similar to the water sounds associated with the caves. The water in the fountain also produced a high level of humidity, like that in the caves. I then remembered being told that the humidity in the caves approximated 85 per-cent...it was all coming together now! He added that fruit would be left in birdhouses to attract the birds. As it decayed, the insects generated from it and attracted to it provided a readily available food supply—additional incen-tive for the birds to settle there. Guano and ammonia spread on the floor would convince the birds that other birds had already chosen this location for their nests. Once the house was established, the excess guano would be used to initiate other birdhouses or sold as highly valued fertilizer to farmers. I then realized that the lack of guano on the city streets was due to its concentration within the birdhouses—another advantage to both birds and humans.

Back in Kuala Lumpur, I reviewed my research. Malaysia answers 20 percent of the international demand for bird's nests, with the southern city of Kuching processing over 80 percent of the nests collected worldwide. We now had first-hand knowledge of this process. Indonesia, a close neighbour, answers another 50 percent of the international demand. I would therefore return to Indonesia, this time to research food produced from an animal's front end rather than its rear. After spending the night in Kuala Lumpur, we flew to Padang, the provincial capital located on the western side of the island of Sumatra in Indonesia. It is an important seaport from which Indonesia's coffee, rubber, tobacco, spices, and cement are exported all over the globe.

From Padang we made our way north to Budda Tenghi. This city was, and is, officially known as the capital of the bird's nest trade on the large island of Sumatra. Here, we met a bird's nest dealer, one of the few big operators on the island. I was surprised to see how open he was to my many questions, until I discovered that he had lived for several years in the United States. He agreed to take us to one of the largest caves on the island. Before setting off, we stopped at the dealer's home for a meal.

Once again, as in Malaysia, I had to don my protective equipment and clothing for another long hike. Indeed, it was a very long trip for us, but one that was necessary in light of the importance this place in Indonesia holds in the edible bird's-nest market. We travelled for many long hours on the congested roads leading up to the cave, and during the journey I heard repeatedly that, like Kuching in Malaysia, Budda Tenghi had been Indonesia's edible bird's-nest capital for decades.

We travelled kilometre after kilometre along the winding roads nestled into the hilly regions surrounding Budda Tenghi. The vegetation was rich and tropical, and the occasional rain produced a thick fog, reducing visibility on the road. I kept wondering what new things we would discover here, and what differences there would be between these caves and the ones we had explored on the island of Borneo. For some reason I felt more anxious on this trip than I had during my travels in Malaysia. I relived many uneasy memories of my night-time adventures during my previous visit to Indonesia, dodging corrupt officials in search of Kopi Luwak coffee. This time, thankfully, our trip was surprisingly uneventful as the police calmly waved us through each checkpoint. In a barely audible whisper I asked the guide why we were always given such quick clearance. His whispered answer was that we were dealing with one of the largest and best-known dealers on the island, and that no one would dare to stop him for any reason. What a difference a little influence makes!

Finally, we came to a dirt road and the dealer told us that we were very close. When the road ended, we walked to our destination in the warm tropical rain, sometimes wading through knee-high water to attain a distant slope. Eventually, we reached a series of wooden boats tied together. Crossing the rain-swollen river was difficult and dangerous, despite the line that had been attached to propel the boat to the other side without being swept away by the raging waters. While in the boat, it was one person's job to bail the water that made its way in so we would not sink or get our gear soaked. Reaching the far-off shore, we were greeted by bird's nest collectors and others who acted as guards and vigilantes to protect the caves from looting.

From there we were escorted to yet another set of boats. These were moored at the mouth of the cave, since the entire cave was full of water. We boarded the boats, sat down, and then they moved deep into the darkness of the cave. Occasionally, one of the cave climbers would leave the boat to climb the cliff walls while pulling the boat deeper into the cave with a rope. At times, I was told, the water was over sixty metres deep. We were shrouded in darkness but could hear the echo-locating sounds of the swiftlets in the upper reaches of the cave. There were hundreds of birds nesting high on the cave walls. Again we took photos and collected data and samples for later study.

Floating through that cave gave me the fright of my life. Falling into the water would have been fatal. In the darkness, it would have been impossible to find the way out, and the steep sides would have allowed no rest. It was a relief to stand on *terra firma* again.

After leaving the cave, we returned to the dealer's home, where we saw sacks upon sacks full of collected nests. I remember thinking that I must be in the Fort Knox of the bird's nest trade. I again was informed that Indonesia supplied about 50 percent of the world's supply of raw bird's nests but that little processing was actually done in the country. As 80 percent of the processing was done in Malaysia, the nests had to be exported to the island of Borneo to the city of Kuching that I had visited earlier.

While at the dealer's house, I witnessed a bird's nest processor purchase approximately seventy kilograms of raw bird's nest from the dealer. He had two empty luggage cases with him that he stuffed full with the nests he had just purchased, all for cash! Considering the price for each kilogram of nest, this was a large amount of money. I asked my guide the reason the buyer was using luggage instead of shipping containers to take the nests back with him to Kuching for processing. My guide took me aside and explained that a high percentage of the nests were smuggled into Malaysia in order to avoid the import tariff levied by the Malaysian government. "But this is illegal," I said in a whisper, to which my guide answered that it was a very common practice. When I asked what would happen if the smuggler was caught, my guide replied that the smuggler would either pay the penalty or try to bribe the customs officer to let him through.

I thought all of this was very strange. I had heard on the plane during an earlier trip to Kuala Lumpur, the Malaysian capital, that the penalty for smuggling drugs into the country was death. How could it be that customs officers who were so strict with so-called drugs could be bribed to turn a blind eye to smuggling of other types of products? If they could not be trusted in small ways, how could they be trusted in larger matters? I wondered if the Malaysian government knew this was happening. Knowledge of what was going on sent chills up and down my spine. For the second time on this trip I had seen the seedy underworld associated with this trade. First I had been exposed to deliberate product adulteration, and now to international smuggling. I thought to myself that I had led a sheltered life as a scientist, not realizing what intrigue surrounded the food delicacies I studied.

After a brief chat with this dealer we returned to Padang, where we caught a flight to Kuala Lumpur, Malaysia, and finally to Hong Kong, the final stop in my journey. On the plane to Hong Kong I mulled over all the different experiences I had had in Malaysia and Indonesia. Both countries had helped me to piece together the edible bird's-nest trade—Indonesia as the biggest supplier of raw bird's nests and Malaysia as the largest processor. Now it was time to go to Hong Kong, the main global distribution hub for edible bird's nests. Even North America, the world's second-largest importer of edible bird's nests, uses Hong Kong as an intermediary. Hong Kong, then, would be my main source for technical information about the nests, and I was determined to learn whatever I could.

Upon arrival, we travelled through crowded streets to various shops and warehouse centres in the heart of Hong Kong where thousands of commercial edible bird's-nest products were sold, housed, or shipped. Hong Kong is where most of the nests from various global locations are centralized, packaged, and redistributed worldwide.

I took numerous photos, notes, and samples, and also had the opportunity to speak to many shopkeepers and traditional medical practitioners. In Eastern medicine, many foods are believed to possess medicinal properties, and the nests are no exception. They told me of the nests' many health benefits. From anecdotal evidence, they could be used for everything from lung infections to purifying the skin. I was told that some people consumed this product as a cure for AIDS, while others used it as a cure for cancer.

My days in Hong Kong passed all too quickly, and before I knew it I had boarded a plane back to Canada. The next stop would be Vancouver, and then finally Toronto. From there I would soon be home—only to embark upon my next adventure, this time in my research laboratory.

I was eager to begin working on all the samples I had collected and to sift through all the photos and notes. Within a day of my return I was in the laboratory to begin working on the nests I had procured in Malaysia, Indonesia, and Hong Kong. Since little is known about the composition of these nests, my investigation had to be methodical. I wanted to discover if there was any substantial chemical difference between the "lower" grade white nests and the premium red blood nests. In addition, due to the recent rise in the adulteration rate of these nests, it was imperative to develop relatively rapid, simple, effective, and reliable analytical methods that could be used in the field to detect possible anomalies at much earlier stages in the distribution chain.

I conducted various tests on both nest types to determine their respective compositions. Both nests contained (from lowest to highest) an identical order of lipid, ash, carbohydrate, and protein. By far the most abundant component in both nest types was crude protein, at about 63 percent. In addition, both nests contained a common protein that is very similar in molecular weight to the highly allergenic ovotransferrin protein found in eggs. Upon closer examination, it became apparent that this ovotransferrin-like protein was a major constituent of the nest. The sheer volume of the protein negated the idea that its presence might be due to an inadvertent contamination of the nest by a broken egg; ovotransferrin was indeed an integral component of the nest's structural material. Interestingly, the red (terra cotta) colour of the blood nest was very similar to the colour of purified ovotransferrin in its iron-complexed state, whereas the white nest was similar in colour to ovotransferrin in its non-iron-complexed form. This supported the hypothesis that the protein in both nest types was at least ovotransferrin-like, and shared some of the characteristics of ovotransferrin in eggs. Moreover, the difference in the iron contents of both nest types, as indicated by atomic absorption analysis, further supported this hypothesis. Scanning electron microscopy (SEM) combined with X-ray microanalysis performed at various locations on the surface of the red nests indicated relatively high levels of iron compared with the white nests. These analyses also indicated that the distribution of various elements in the nests is highly variable, indicating possible compositional differences in the secreted saliva. I also performed a variety of tests to determine if any hemoglobin (blood) was present in the red "blood" nest—a claim made by all in the bird's nest trade and those who consume them. The results were clear: absolutely no hemoglobin was found!

Since proteins were found to be the major constituent of both nest types, it is not surprising that several medical studies have shown a severe allergic reaction among some young children who consumed bird's nest soup. The descriptions of these reactions were similar to those induced by egg-like proteins. In North America, as well as in the rest of the world, however, there is no or very little information as to how many children have experienced bird's nest–induced anaphylaxis. The medical community may not even be aware of its existence or properly trained to diagnose it.

Practitioners of traditional Chinese medicine have consistently insisted that the consumption of bird's nest soup is beneficial for treating a variety of health problems. As I was informed in Hong Kong, it is often administered to elderly and very young persons who are recovering from various types of infections. Interestingly, studies have indicated that ovotransferrin from eggs is both bacteriostatic (inhibiting the growth of bacteria) and bactericidal (destroying bacteria) in nature. It would follow that if the protein identified in these nests was in fact an ovotransferrin-like protein, then it could have significant infection-fighting properties. This may be the reason the bird's nest soup has historically played such an important role in traditional Chinese medicine.

The salivary nest cement is the most important ingredient in the edible bird's nest and is undoubtedly one of the most expensive food ingredients in the world. I learned on my trip that nests that were adulterated with *Tremella* fungus, karaya gum, or red seaweed were relatively low in overall crude protein compared with the 63 percent crude protein found in pure white bird nest material. Therefore, comparison of the total protein content of suspected adulterated nests with the pure edible nest could potentially be used as one of a number of tests to confirm authenticity.

Preliminary visual tests revealed detectable differences between genuine and adulterated bird's nests. When pieces of adulterated nests containing karaya gum, red seaweed, and *Tremella* fungus treated with concentrated nitric acid were presented to panellists, their presence could be detected. The panellists also noted that the unadulterated (pure) nest was much darker in colour than the adulterated ones due to the higher protein content.

My bird's nest adventure was an incredible experience. I had braved gangsters, crocodiles, rainforests, vicious guard dogs, smugglers, and (former) headhunters, but the knowledge I had gained was invaluable. Bird's nest soup may indeed perform as advertised. As if to emphasize this, my antique metal nest-harvesting tool sits in my office, a constant reminder of the value of ancient lore.

Leaning back in my office chair one day, my eyes again fell on the tool, and I pondered the unique process that transformed a bird's saliva into an expensive and sought-after food delicacy. At first glance it seemed very unusual, but then again, so would honey, considering that it is actually the regurgitated product from the bee's honey stomach. This line of thought led to *Chicha*, another regurgitated product, but this time by humans. In Peru and Bolivia, this alcoholic beverage is made by people who chew maize and spit it into a large container. The saliva mixes with the maize and starts to break down the starch into simple sugars which then, and only then, are available for yeasts to use as food for their growth and reproduction. The yeast processes the partially digested maize sugars, producing alcohol as a by-product. Yum! It is also known that in some cultures mothers would pre-chew their infant's food...no Gerber baby foods there. This phenomenon also happens in the animal world where the male penguin ingests, digests, and regurgitates its food for its young ever growing, and always hungry chick.

Maybe, just maybe, this type of special processing is not as unusual as one might think!

A typical Moroccan grinding stone used to express the oil from the argan seed. Many of these grinding stones are old, being handed down from one generation to the next.

A typical Moroccan salad prepared with freshly chopped tomatoes, onions, peppers, and lettuce. The final touch to the salad is a light drizzle with precious and delicious argan oil.

Camel meat, an important source of animal protein, hanging for sale at a typical local outdoor butcher in Morocco. These meats are, at times, cooked at adjacent outdoor restaurants while the customer waits.

Dr. Marcone collects an edible bird's nest attached to the wall of a limestone cave in Malaysia. The ancient collection tool used was given to him as a gift by his guide when visiting the graves of bird's nest collectors in a Niah cave on the island of Borneo.

The chemical treatment of collected birds' nests to facilitate the loosening of the fine feathers, down, and other debris prior to manual cleaning by process workers using tweezers and other tools.

Process workers cleaning and processing raw birds' nests in Kuching, Malaysia using a variety of instruments including tweezers to remove bird feathers and other debris from the softened nests.

The alignment of strands of cleaned birds' nests in a pre-shaped metal form. This is followed by drying, packaging and then exported for sale around the world.

A very expensive spoonful of edible bird's nest soup teeming with several strands of the bird nest material. A bowl such as this can cost as much as (US) $80–$100.

An excited Dr. Marcone discovers the existence of a hamlet in Italy bearing his family's name. Tradition maintains that it was established by a viscount bearing the surname Marcone who lived in this region during the Middle Ages. This was much to Dr. Marcone's surprise, and delight!

Casu Frazigu (Marzu) cheese (a.k.a. maggot cheese) being inoculated by the special fly during storage in a secret underground facility. The fly enters through ventilation holes, and lays its eggs in the cracks on the surface of the cheese within the first two to three days after forming.

The traditional way of serving Casu Frazigu (Marzu). This pungent viscous cheese with wiggling maggots is usually spread on a traditional Sardinian flatbread and enjoyed with a glass of full-bodied red wine.

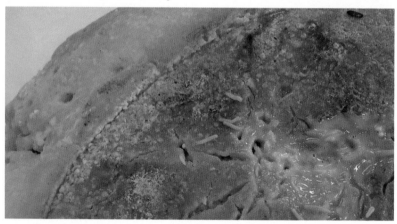

Casu Frazigu (Marzu) cheese with the typical transparent maggots found throughout the cheese. These maggots are responsible for breaking down the fats and proteins in the milk that produce the desirable characteristic rotten odour, and taste.

A morel mushroom nestled in the forest debris under the shadow of a poplar tree.

Collected morels are counted and recorded by the judges at the 45th Annual Morel Mushroom Hunt and Competition held in mid-May at the height of the morel season in Boyne City, Michigan U.S.A.

A typical way of preparing and enjoying *escamoles* (a.k.a. ant egg caviar), which is scooped up with a piece of crisp tortilla.

Dr. Marcone cautiously consumes his first bite of *escamoles* in a restaurant in Mexico City.

Dr. Marcone holds a live poisonous scorpion that is typically found in open market places throughout Asia. Scorpions such these are consumed in various soups that are deemed to have medicinal properties.

A very expensive dish consisting of scorpions and crocodile meat, which is served in many countries throughout Asia with some minor variations.

Dr. Marcone consumes a scorpion with absolutely no hesitation whatsoever. It tastes like crabmeat, not chicken.

The bottom of a bucket with hundreds of poisonous scorpions sold for consumption in an open market in Asia. Soup made from these scorpions is believed to have medicinal properties.

A steaming plate of sautéed water beetles, a typical dish in many Asian countries.

Dr. Marcone is seen looking for his dinner in a typical Asian market in China. A large variety of insects as well as other unusual animals such as snakes are offered for sale. Dinner anyone?

ITALY (SARDINIA AND ABRUZZI)

CASU FRAZIGU (MARZU): THE WORLD'S ENIGMATIC AND UNDERGROUND CHEESE, A.K.A. ROTTEN OR MAGGOT CHEESE

My adventures had taken me to exotic locations, many of which had been previously unexplored by food scientists. I had travelled from the rainforests of Indonesia to the savannahs of Ethiopia to study Kopi Luwak coffee, to the semi-arid regions of Morocco in search of argan oil, and all over the rainforests, caves, and metropolitan cities of Southeast Asia to research edible bird's nests. Many of the foods I studied in my travels had developed in large part due to the isolation of the culture that produced them. I was comfortable with this hypothesis until the day I heard of a certain cheese called Casu Frazigu, or "rotten cheese" or "maggot cheese."

Until the moment Casu Frazigu intruded upon my consciousness, my day had progressed like any other as I answered the myriad of emails, checked on the students in one of my distance education courses, and spoke with a steady stream of both graduate and undergraduate students who had come to ask every question imaginable under God's heaven. Oddly enough, I always seem to learn the most from the students who ask the most bizarre, outlandish questions! With them and through them, my envelope of comfort is expanded as they constantly challenge me to see things differently. I have learned, and continue to learn, so much from them. It is role reversal in the best sense: the students become teachers and the teacher becomes a student, creating an incredible and fruitful relationship.

It was on one of these ordinary, uneventful days when a graduate student named Hamid, someone whom I consider a trusted friend, walked into the lab. Little did I know he was bringing news of one of the oddest and most gut-wrenching food delicacies I had ever heard about. So much for my ordinary day!

Hamid informed me about a cheese called Casu Frazigu, a very unusual cheese as it has thousands of maggots in it which, by the way, are consumed along with the cheese. My mind wandered off to the pleasures of distant rainforests and savannahs, wondering what could possess anyone to eat such a thing. Much to my surprise, I was told that the cheese was made and eaten in Italy, one of the cultural capitals of the world. Despite my hope that this would turn out to be a mere urban legend, my Italian mother confirmed the tale adding that my grandfather was quite a connoisseur of this delicacy. She remembered him eating this cheese shortly after the Second World War, in or around 1947. In fact, my mother recalled thinking it was rather good on the one occasion she tasted it, though she was only about ten years old at the time and did not remember it that clearly. Was her memory suppressing the more unpleasant aspects? I will never know. Further, she told me that the cheese was produced in the mountains that surrounded their village of Villa Santa Maria.

When I talked with my friend Sylvie, an Italian journalist who had written several stories about my research work, she explained that Casu Frazigu was indeed a famous Italian cheese. Its sale was illegal, but it was often served at weddings and other special occasions. She said that it had originated on the island of Sardinia and had extremely deep roots on the island. I informed her that it had also been produced in the province of Abruzzi where my parents were born and raised. To this she replied that it had probably spread to Abruzzi from Sardinia...its journey being clouded by the mist of time.

Fascinated both by the cheese itself and by my ancestral connection with it, I asked Sylvie if she could help me find this highly prized but illegal delicacy. A few days later she emailed telling me that a gentleman in Sardinia had assured her that he could get the cheese for me to study. The peak season for ripened Casu Frazigu, also known as Casu Marzu, was during the months of July and August. I decided to fly there to meet with him as soon as possible. Sylvie said that her editor wanted her to do a story on both this famous but outlawed cheese as well as the Canadian researcher who was studying it. No problem, I responded. It was the least I could do in return for her arranging this visit and putting me in touch with a person who could get me some of Italy's top-secret cheese.

The flight from Rome to Alghero, a town on the island of Sardinia, landed me at one of the smallest airports I had ever seen. The plane landed, taxied right up to the terminal doors, and let us disembark. We walked from the plane into the terminal as one would walk from your car into your home. In fact, the plane was much larger than the building itself! I laughed to myself when I recalled my concern that

Sylvie and I would miss each other at the airport. As I walked off the plane, I saw her and a gentleman whom she introduced as Torre.

Torre was a retired linguistics professor whose command of the Italian language was impeccable. I was embarrassed by my Italian, having learned it from my parents as a second language but Torre was gracious and made me feel comfortable almost immediately. I admired him tremendously, and he soon became my mentor. He had studied and taught languages and literature in the city of Sassari for many years. Since 1975, he had worked with the local government to promote Sardinian culture. He had also worked with different governmental groups to convince the Italian government to recognize *Il sardo* as the official language of Sardinia. Torre informed me that *Il sardo* was a separate language, not a dialect, and was officially recognized as such in 1997. As of 1999, any individual could write and petition the government in the language. Predating the Italian language by several centuries, *Il sardo* is very close to Latin, but when I heard Torre speak to his housekeeper in *Il sardo,* I could not understand a single word.

That evening, we had a special dinner in a penthouse restaurant in the middle of Sassari, or "Tattari" in *Il sardo*. Torre informed me that he had something waiting for me in his flat that I would find most interesting but would not tell me what it was. Arrangements had been made for us to visit the University of Sassari to speak to some of the researchers there who would be able to help me in my work. Sylvie, who had to fly back to Milan in two days, also decided to accompany us. She wanted to interview me, not only about the work that I would be performing on this cheese but also with regard to my edible bird's-nest research, the results of which would soon be published in a peer-reviewed scientific journal called *Food Research International.*

After dinner, we made our way to Torre's flat, where Sylvie and I would stay during our visit to Sassari. Since the flat was within walking distance of the university and the other cultural areas of the city, being based there would facilitate my research on the cheese. As Torre had another flat a short distance away, he would stay there so I could work undisturbed.

Immediately upon opening the door to the flat, Sylvie exclaimed, "I can smell it!" As we got closer, the smell became stronger. My heart started to beat faster as we neared the kitchen. Was the famous, prohibited cheese waiting for me? At that point, neither legality nor odour mattered.

Torre unwrapped two separate containers, revealing two cheese wheels for me to test. Fascinating! The clicking sounds of the thousands of maggots hitting the sides of the containers had been audible from a distance of six metres. And the strong odour emanating from the cheese was distinct from several rooms away.

Torre said that we needed to place the cheese on the balcony to keep it at the right temperature. I inquired what would happen if a cat happened by during the night and stole the cheese that I had travelled all the way from Canada to study. Sylvie, in a funny but sarcastic way, reminded me that we were on the fifth floor of the building. It would be unusual to have "cat burglars" at such a height. Anyway, she added, no cat in its right mind would eat cheese that reeked like this! Even cats that eat garbage have their limits! Torre indicated where on the balcony we should put the cheese to keep it in a cool spot. Sylvie protested that the cheese would be too close to her bedroom window and that she did not want to get "gassed" during the night. We eventually found a location with which we could all live.

That night, as I slept on the sofa with the balcony doors wide open, I could hear raindrops hitting my precious cheese. I quickly rose and ran to the balcony to rescue the cheese only to discover that there were no raindrops. The "drops" hitting the bag were actually the maggots jumping and hitting the inside of the container.

I went back to bed and listened to my maggots. It was like listening to a baby's breath on the baby monitor. I was reminded of the night during my Ethiopian adventure when I had slept with my Kopi Luwak samples in my jacket to protect them from the bold, oversized cockroaches. It dawned on me that my zealous protection of samples of rare foods established a close bond between me and the foods I studied. To me, food was not merely sustenance, but something more: it was a vibrant, evolving piece of history, and my job was to unlock its secrets.

Early the next morning, we made our way to the University of Sassari where we met three young scientists and talked about Casu Frazigu cheese. Marco, Giovanni, and Nicoletta, though young, were among the most intelligent and wonderful people I have ever met. They told me that shepherds traditionally made the cheese from milk collected from their sheep. The cheese was usually produced in May and aged in areas open to the elements. As the cheese aged, a certain fly called *Piophila casei* (not the domestic housefly) would deposit its eggs in the various fissures that formed in the cheese. If the surface of the cheese became too dry or hard, or did not have adequate fissures, these flies could not deposit their eggs within the cheese. If the flies were successful, the larvae would develop and start moving through the cheese excreting all sorts of digestive enzymes as they made their way through. This gave the cheese a creamy texture, similar to the common Camembert. Cheese that became infested by common housefly maggots is completely inedible. The special "fly cheese" produced smaller maggots which excreted chemicals that transformed the cheese into something which was highly prized.

The researchers informed me that the cheese was edible only for a very short period from late July to mid-August. Judging when the cheese was past its prime was difficult, even for those who traditionally produced it. It was for this reason that the Italian government had outlawed it and would not recognize it as a saleable, legitimate Sardinian cheese. Although it was not legal for sale, production continued throughout the island. Casu Frazigu had been produced and consumed for centuries. Interestingly, there were very few reported cases of people becoming ill after the consumption of this particular cheese. When I asked if the researchers themselves had ever eaten the cheese, I got enthusiastic affirmative answers. It was a customary part of family gatherings, baptisms, weddings, and all other special occasions. Even as microbiologists with Ph.D.s, they had no underlying concerns regarding this cheese, having eaten it since childhood. Some things are stronger than education.

The researchers kindly offered to let me use their facilities to study these cheeses, rather than my taking the chance that the cheese, with such a short shelf life, would be past its prime by the time I took it back to Canada for testing in my laboratory. I was to return the following day with the cheeses Torre had acquired for me, to begin the microbiological tests.

Later that afternoon, Torre asked if we would like to take a short drive to Bosa to see the coast. While driving, he told me a great deal about the Sardinian culture and language so I could better understand the historical and cultural background of the cheese. In Bosa, I walked the streets asking different shopkeepers about the cheese. Everyone acknowledged its existence, but none would say anything about where one might purchase it. Torre informed me that most people with whom I spoke would either be able to purchase the cheese or have a family member who made it and would give it to them. Disclosing more to a stranger was risky.

Francesco, an architect, told me that his father had eaten this type of cheese twenty-five years ago in Naples, and that he did not think it was produced solely in Sardinia. This was important, as I wanted to find out the source of the cheese my grandfather and mother had eaten in 1947. At times my work seems closer to that of a detective than a food scientist. I travel the world in search of new, interesting, and unusual food delicacies. In my travels I am constantly looking for new leads to follow and rushing off to see if they will pan out. I interview people, cross-reference sources and resources, and try to piece everything together. It is like assembling an enormous, immensely complex jigsaw puzzle. I have to think on my feet and be ready to move or act very quickly indeed.

That same afternoon, Sylvie set up her recording equipment and interviewed me about my trip and the past research I had conducted on the edible bird's nest. We worked quickly to cover all the possible aspects of the interview as Sylvie had to catch a flight to Milan. When we dropped her at the airport that evening, I had a tear in my eye as I said goodbye. "Sylvie," I said, "if it had not been for you, I would not be here to research this cheese." She looked back at me and said, "The rest is yours! Enjoy what you are doing—I can see that you are passionate about all that you do!"

The following day, I returned to the university with the two cheeses that Torre had obtained for me. As Marco cut them open to prepare them for the battery of tests we would perform, thousands of maggots began appearing and crawling all over the lab bench. It was an unbelievable sight! Some of them even jumped on my camera as I snapped photographs while I later found others in my hair.

The test tubes were prepared and the selective media plates were made, ready to be inoculated with our cheeses. I was extremely excited that we had accomplished so much in a day, but with four seasoned researchers working in unison I could expect no less. After we completed the tests, the seventy-two-hour incubation began. This gave me time to do my other research work.

In order to learn more about food in Sardinia, and Casu Frazigu in particular, I visited the Giovanni Antonio Sunne Archaeological Museum in Sassari. Cultural research is essential for food scientists, particularly those like me who study rare foods. Food scientists do more than analyze foods for safety and nutritional content—we study all aspects of a culture to come up with a complete food profile. Origins and historical development are critical pieces of the puzzle. At the museum, I was able to visit a special collection called Cibi e Sapori nell'Italia Antica, "Foods and Flavours of Ancient Italy." This exhibit helped explain the origin of edible rotten cheese.

I learned that the first human traces in Sardinia date from the Palaeolithic period, or the Old Stone Age. Flint tools from the low Palaeolithic period (about five hundred thousand years ago) had been found at various sites, and the earliest human remains found on the island have been carbon dated to be over one hundred thousand years old. To my surprise, the original Sardinians predated all Italian peninsular inhabitants. I knew then that I was dealing with a very distinct and ancient people and culture. More importantly, I learned that Sardinia had been exporting food, and probably their eating habits, to other parts of the known world for at least two thousand years. I had seen paintings dating from the first century AD that depict ships transporting food from Sardinia. Did the custom of making and eating Casu Frazigu cheese first get transferred to the mainland of Italy at that time, or was it simply an imported delicacy, made on the island and transported to the peninsula? This was of particular interest to me in my quest to discover how my grandfather might have eaten this cheese after the Second World War in the very distinctive region of Abruzzi on the Italian peninsula.

My examination of the displayed prehistoric artefacts revealed that, prior to the export of food and eating practices by the ancient Sardinians, the Sardinians had produced advanced cooking utensils, at least since the Palaeolithic period. Early on, the Sardinians seem to have had a very well established and developed culture that emphasized the importance of food, food preservation, and the advancement of various food practices and production methods. It was likely in this context that Casu Frazigu was developed. Interestingly enough, my interviews with various linguists and cultural experts indicated that Sardinians have always had a fear of the sea. Sardinians do not generally describe the sea as calm or benevolent. These negative associations were further evidenced by the fact that almost every "coastal" city in Sardinia that I visited was approximately one to three kilometres inland from the coast. And although Sardinia is an island surrounded by a sea rich in fish, I found that, historically, Sardinians have not been very fond of seafood. I was able to verify these findings independently. Because the sea had not historically provided food, the people of Sardinia developed advanced agricultural practices early on, one of these being the rearing of a variety of domestic animals for food and food by-products. Today, as in the past, the island is covered in sheep, and cheese made from sheep's milk, like Casu Frazigu, is very common. Fear of the sea and the emphasis on agricultural practices led to the production of cheese—in particular, the production and love of rotten cheese. Casu Frazigu, then, was not an anomaly or a freak occurrence, but something that had been deliberately developed and consumed for centuries.

Three days had passed, and all the microbiological plates and test tubes were brought out to be examined and the results tabulated. What we found was astonishing. The rotten, maggoty cheeses we had tested were not only safe to eat but had microbiological counts and microbial species similar to those of other cheeses that did not contain maggots. For this to be true, however, it was crucial to begin the process of making Casu Frazigu with a good starting cheese, that is one that had not been contaminated by bad microorganisms prior to the deposit of the fly eggs. We concluded that the maggots found in the cheeses did not render the final product inferior in any way whatsoever (as some might believe), but instead created a product fundamentally different from the starting cheese. The final rotten cheese, in other words, was a unique food, and had to be judged on its own merits rather than by pre-existing standards.

With these results in mind, we brought the cheeses up to the sensory testing area where members of the department had eagerly gathered. It was there that I saw how the cheeses were consumed with the Sardinians' special flatbreads and red wine. Since the results showed that the cheeses were fine to eat, I did something that many would find hard to believe: I scooped a tiny piece of the cheese, maggots and all, placed it on the flatbread, and put it into my mouth—bread, cheese, and maggots...I ate it all! I felt as though I had been initiated into a unique and special cheese connoisseur community.

The Sardinian press had caught wind of my visit, and before I knew it, they had found out where I was staying. Somehow they had figured out that Torre, as a promoter of Sardinian culture, had something to do with my visit, and they interviewed me the next day. An article appeared in the next day's newspaper complete with photo, declaring to the world that Casu Frazigu cheese had been shown to be safe to eat. I had sparked an island-wide debate on the right of the Italian government to involve itself in internal decisions regarding foods. The debate raged on even as I left the island, one article demanding that Berlusconi's government base its policies on scientific fact rather than on public perception. There's nothing like going out in style!

After leaving Sardinia for Rome, I had planned to travel to my ancestral hometown, Villa Santa Maria located in the region of Abruzzi east of Rome. At the Leonardo da Vinci International Airport in Rome, I literally had to run with my luggage in tow to what seemed like the farthest corner of the airport to catch the train into central Rome. My luggage seemed to become heavier and heavier with every corridor I ran down and the more I ran, the farther away the train seemed! Perhaps I should require my graduate students to pass a yearly physical fitness test in preparation for the rigours of a career in food science. It was important for me to catch the train to Stazione Termini, Rome's central train station where I hoped to connect with the train to Abruzzi.

The ride to Stazione Termini took approximately forty minutes and was most uncomfortable as we were crowded in like sardines. You could not have squeezed another person in with a shoehorn, even if everybody had sucked in and had held their breath. Never in my life had I seen more people in one spot. Arriving in Stazione Termini, I quickly retrieved the second train ticket from my overstuffed bag. I had purchased it in Sardinia with the intention of saving time, just in case I had to rush as I was now doing. It was an open ticket but all the delays in transit had made me extremely late, and I arrived just minutes before the last train departed. If I had missed that one, I would have had to spend the night in Rome—which, under other circumstances, would have been an attractive option. Given my mission, though, I was anxious to reach my final destination before putting my head on the pillow in a deep and well deserved restful slumber.

While waiting for the train, I realized just how exhausted I was and I just stood on the platform, motionless. I just happened to glance at the front page of a newspaper in a box. It was a report on the recent (July 7, 2005) bombings in the London subways that had killed fifty-two people while injuring over seven hundred. In a tired daze, I read how Italian authorities were stepping up security in all subway and train stations, and especially in the one where I was now standing, Stazione Termini. The story indicated that there were good reasons to believe an attack might occur.

My heart began to pound and my throat tightened. I had had too many near misses in the past to take this information with any degree of equanimity. I tried putting the matter out of my thoughts by concentrating on a group of young people who had just arrived on the platform. They were happy and full of life, speaking about their summer holidays and their vacation on the Adriatic coast. Young people with their enthusiasm and *joie de vivre* have a way of living in the moment, whereas people like me are always racing through the present to something in the future thus missing out on the moment. We ought to remember what it was like to be young, and keep in mind that the "present" is just that—a gift of the moment. The past cannot be changed, the future is still unknown.

I had just finished reflecting on this when their conversation changed to the recent bombings and a voice repeated what the Italian authorities were saying—that Italy might be the next target. Although these people were full of life, this tragedy affected them too, causing them to wonder about the chances that they could become unwitting victims.

I boarded the train and decided to stay in the non-air-conditioned coach as there were no other people in it. Surely the terrorists would not bomb an empty wagon, I thought! Looking in my luggage, I located the Casu Frazigu cheese samples, and took them out to examine them and to see how they had survived the trip so far. I shrugged off my gloomy thoughts by thinking that, if such an attack did occur, I would be covered in maggots from the cheese I was holding before I even had time to hit the ground. What a thought indeed!

Critters such as the maggots in this cheese and the leeches that are used in some medical treatments may sound revolting to some, but they have their uses. Leeches and maggots have served medical purposes for centuries. Countless wounded soldiers, barely clinging to life in the trenches, avoided gangrenous infections thanks to the maggots that kept their wounds clean by feasting on the decaying tissue. Doctors have deliberately placed leeches on surface wounds to clean them, and in the ear canal to help treat infections. Perhaps, I thought, the maggots in the cheese serve a similar preserving or cleansing purpose. Reflecting on the curative properties of leeches, my mind was occupied with something constructive and not with things over which I had no control.

The train ride gave me a lot of time to reflect on the Casu Frazigu cheese and to wonder if the cheese my grandfather and mother had eaten in 1947 had come from

Sardinia or been produced locally in Abruzzi. We were crossing the Apennine Mountains, and many of the roads I saw from the train were only built after the Second World War. Many of the smaller roads that existed previously were either severely damaged or impassable after the war. So how did the cheese make its way from Sardinia into Rome, the only open port on the peninsula, and then across to Abruzzi? I asked many questions and found few answers.

I made my way to the village of Villa Santa Maria, the place of my ancestral roots and the birthplace of my parents, Lidia and Domenico, and also of my grandfather Guiseppe, the patriarch of the family. This small village, nestled within the mountains of Abruzzo, would serve as my home during my work. Each time I had visited the place of my origins, I learned more of who I was and what has made me who I am today. My uncle Guido and aunt Maria greeted me with wide outstretched arms, a smile wider than their arms, and with a joyful tone in their greetings. They were, and continue to be, my second set of parents. Not too many people can brag of having two sets of loving parents. I am very grateful to God that He has blessed me so!

Villa Santa Maria is also known as Patria dei Cuochi, or the "Homeland of Chefs," as a saint by the name of San Francesco Cararciolo established a school for chefs in the city over five hundred years ago. He is known as the patron saint and protector of chefs around the world. San Francesco Cararciolo's story is incredible, and in some respects I was following in his footsteps. I went to the chapel that houses his relics and prayed before the sanctuary that I would be guided and helped to find someone who could assist me in my Casu Frazigu research. Afterwards, I proceeded to the city hall, where I discovered much to my surprise that the mayor had been expecting me. Were the newspapers to blame? I will never know.

At the culinary school, my prayer for help was answered. Antonio, a famous master chef and retired professor, was a font of cheese knowledge. He was probably the only person left in the city who really knew anything about Casu Frazigu. I learned that it has many names: Casu Frazigu in Sardinia, Casu Marchetto ("slightly rotten cheese") in Abruzzi, and Casu Puntato ("cheese with little holes"—maggot holes).

The next day my uncle and I took a trip through the beautiful mountains of Abruzzi, moving from elevations of 386 metres to 1,280 above sea level, and encountering the most dramatic change in temperature I have ever experienced. We finally made it to Aversa degli Abruzzi (580 above sea level) and, after much searching, found the Bio Agriturismo ("bio-agricultural tourism centre"). Here, a man named Nuncio informed us that "rotten or maggot cheese" did not originate in Sardinia but rather in Abruzzi. This is where the war over who claims the rights to the origin of this cheese begins! Nuncio's method of making Casu Frazigu does not utilize maggots, and after testing both the maggot cheese in Sardinia and this (legal) cheese in Abruzzi, I can say that there are very few differences in flavour.

While searching for the location where this specialty cheese is made, we got a little lost and ended up in a city called Cocullo. Like my ancestral town, Cocullo has a patron saint, but theirs is San Domenico, protector of the people from snakes. In fact, I was told that people celebrate the birth of their protector by wearing a live snake around their neck—venom sac removed, off course. "Wow," I thought, "this country is full of surprises." Little did I know that the biggest surprise was still to come!

As we drove back to Villa Santa Maria, I stared out the window at the magnificent scenery and the people going about their business in the fields, on the streets, in the shops and cafés, and on the street corners in the small villages through which we passed. My mind drifted from one thing to another and finally settled on my family in Canada. This is what they wanted me to see...it was their gift to me, and I treasure it!

Suddenly we passed a village sign with my surname on it: *Monte Marcone.* I could not believe my eyes! Excitedly, I yelled to my uncle to stop the car and, while he was pulling over, asked him if he had seen the sign we had just passed. Without much fanfare he indicated that he had, and in fact, he said, we were just entering the village of Monte Marcone. This was fabulous as the only Monte I had previously been aware of was Monte Carlo! I got out of the car and walked back to the sign as everyone in the car and on the street watched and wondered what all the excitement was about. I stared at the sign and then snapped a photo of it. My uncle got out of the car and walked up to me, clearly bewildered by my activities. First, I was investigating Casu Frazigu, then I took him on a wild ride through the mountains, and now I was examining some village sign with incongruous enthusiasm.

I asked him if he was aware of this village that bore our family name. "Of course," he said. He had known about it his entire life. He asked me if I would like to return to the car so that we could go home for supper, but I was not going anywhere without learning more about this place. My uncle explained that our family was quite small and that we were most definitely related at some point to the Marcones of this village, and asked me again to please get back into the car...he was hungry and wanted to go home to eat his dinner. Again I told him that I needed to get more information before leaving and asked if they would kindly wait for me by the car. It was an opportunity I was not going to let pass. I was living in the moment, my moment!

I walked into a small smoke shop and found an old lady and her son working there. I asked her if she knew the origins of the village and she told me it was a parcel of land donated to the people in the eighteenth century by a viscount with the surname Marcone. Here I was looking for the origins of maggot cheese and now I had stumbled upon the ancestral origins of my own family, which appeared to include royalty. Laughing to myself, I thought, "Screw the maggot cheese, this find is even more interesting." I never would have thought I would have to research maggot cheese in order to find out about my ancestral roots!

That evening, after a day filled with travelling, adventures, and discovery in the mountains of Abruzzi, I sat in my grandfather Giuseppe's chair at the kitchen table, the very spot where he would have consumed the maggot cheese after World War II. I pulled out my samples and placed them on the table in front of me. I had just re-created the scene that had taken place many times so many decades ago. Finally, the cheese had returned to the very spot in which both my grandfather and my mother had consumed it. It is said that history repeats itself, and in this case it actually did!

I had learned that the maggot cheese that had graced this table so long ago probably had not come from Sardinia after World War II, due to the disrupted state of the transportation corridors that would most certainly have destroyed this very "delicate" cheese. Instead, it likely had its origins in the very foothills and mountains surrounding this beautiful, remote, almost insignificant tiny country village. But even more interesting was that maggot cheese was adamantly claimed by two distinct regions in Italy as being of their own invention, yet at the same time was something "despised"—or so I had been led to believe.

The love-hate relationship with this bizarre food may not be as strange as one might think, and leads us to examine exactly what we feel about other food preferences. In many cases I submit that we too have love-hate relationships. One only needs to look at the contorted faces of people consuming raw oysters or drinking straight tequila (correctly called mescal with a maggot in it) to confirm my hypothesis. The question still remains: Why do we do it?

CANADA AND THE UNITED STATES
THE GREAT NORTH AMERICAN MOREL HUNT

Their secret locations passed down from one aficionado to the next, morels (Morchella) are North America's most highly prized wild mushroom. The morels of North America, like the truffles of Europe, have so far resisted man's efforts to culture them; they must be collected from the wild. The morel is one of the few foods left that man has not been able to tame, culture, and cultivate for himself. Man must therefore step back to a time when he was a hunter-gatherer, and revisit his remote roots. Morels and truffles can only be harvested from the wild at specific times of the year. Morels are harvested in May, whereas the truffle season usually runs from late September to November. The limited supply and perishable nature of morels and truffles make them an eagerly anticipated seasonal delicacy, and one that commands an extremely high price. Fresh morels can retail for over a hundred dollars per pound during the harvesting season, whereas the limited dried products can sell for much, much more.

Monica, a seasoned morel hunter, revealed her prized Canadian morel-hunting site to me as she was about to leave Ontario. She, like most other morel hunters, was very proud of her prime morel-hunting ground and guarded its location without compromise or apology. In the world of morel hunting, there is no such thing as sharing one's site with a fellow hunter. Morel hunters in North America and truffle hunters in Europe have one thing in common: their sport is a very private activity, most often conducted alone. But since Monica was leaving the province, she wanted to make certain that her treasured site, which had brought her so much joy and fulfillment, would be guarded and enjoyed by another trustworthy and equally committed hunter. That hunter was me!

She spent weeks educating me about how to locate these wonderful fungal delicacies. The morels' unique camouflage makes finding them a challenge, but Monica shared with me some secret techniques vital to this special hunt. She taught me to lower my body and look ahead, like an ancient hunter stalking a deer, moose, or elk in the forest. In this case, however, the purpose wasn't to sneak up on the unsuspecting prey, but to lower your gaze so you could see the morel peeking out from underneath leaves and woody debris. Some say that the hunter does not find the morel but, rather, the morel allows itself to be found... or not.

The wily hunter must look for freshly disturbed ground, or ground that is indented and allows for water to flow by. The type of trees in the woods is also extremely important. In the past, morels used to favour growing under Dutch elm trees, but when the spread of Dutch elm disease across North America depleted that tree's population, the morels adapted and "chose" to live in a symbiotic relationship with poplar (*Populus*, L.) and the ash (*Fraxinus*, L.) being related to the olive tree. Additionally, morels need decaying wood to grow and thrive. Look for a decaying stump and you just might find some morels.

When spotting a morel, it must be approached with care, so as not to destroy other morels in the area through excited carelessness. The old saying goes, "Where there is one morel, there should be another close by." Monica advised approaching by walking in a zigzag pattern to see if you can spot other morels nearby. She repeatedly went over this detail with me, making sure that I was ready to assume the responsibility of having my own hunting ground. She swore me to secrecy, requiring me to affirm at every meeting that, as a true morel hunter, I would never reveal the location.

The day finally came for me to take possession of my mushroom spot, which was to be passed along to me in an ancient tradition known only to wild-mushroom aficionados. After a twenty-minute drive beyond the university campus, we approached the city limits. I was told to slow down so that we could sneak into a small parking area just off the side of the road next to a semi-abandoned railway track. Monica informed me that we needed to walk the rest of the way, following the railway tracks into the nearby woods.

As we approached the woods, Monica told me to find a stick long enough to use as a walking stick. I began to wonder where we were going. Was the terrain really that treacherous? Almost reading my mind, she smiled at my puzzlement and asked if I knew what the walking stick was to be used for. I smiled back ruefully, realizing that she was testing me to see what I had gleaned from her instructions about locating these elusive mushrooms. She explained that I would use the stick to push back branches and leaves that could conceal the morels from sight. She instructed me to keep my gaze on the distance so that I did not unwittingly trample the morels.

Far into the woods, Monica told me that we were getting close to the site. I had been looking for the elusive mushroom ever since we entered the woods, so I was a little irritated that she had waited this long to tell me that only a portion of the woods would have the right conditions for the mushrooms to grow. My irritation quickly subsided, however, as she leapt forward and yelled that she had found one. I ran after her and almost fell over her as she bent over to pick the mushroom. I told her to stop so that I could take a photograph.

It poked up over the grass. Monica told me to be careful. "Do you remember what I told you earlier?"

"Yes," I blurted. "Where there is one mushroom, there is another close by."

She spun around, and before I could see what she was doing, she had another morel in her hand. They were beautiful specimens, sponge-like caps with a connected stem. She then cut the mushrooms in half and indicated that I should make a proper identification of them. "Look and make sure there is nothing that resembles cotton in the centre of the mushroom, and that the mushroom cap and stem are connected. If not, this would be the inferior half-morel which isn't nearly as desirable."

Then it was my turn to find one, and with slight trepidation I moved forward. I looked into the distance, as I had been taught. All of a sudden my eyes caught something sticking out from underneath the leaves. Quickly, I moved forward and reached out my hand to remove the leaves and debris in the immediate area. There it was! My very own morel, a lot smaller than the one Monica had found, but a morel just the same. I looked around as I had been instructed, and there was a second, and then a third. Yelping in amazement, Monica ran forward, reaching out her hand to see what I had. The smile of approval on her face said it all. She had officially transferred her morel area and her accumulated knowledge to the newest morel hunter: me.

I pointed out that my morels were smaller than hers, but that finding them was more difficult and should count as a bonus for me. She broke out in a loud laugh and said that I was quite correct. She then informed me that I must learn to pinch the mushroom right at the soil level so as not to disturb the mycelium layer just below the soil, since that would stop another mushroom from growing. Moreover, getting extra soil into our mushroom bag would make the mushrooms harder to clean.

For the next two hours, we happily hunted morels. Once, I found a false morel, or half-morel, which Monica used as a teaching moment to instruct me about what to avoid. "These are considered bad. Never eat them or you can become extremely sick." I assured her that I understood. As the sun started to dim, we picked our last morel. We had harvested seventy-six in all... an awaiting feast.

We made our way back to her place, where we would prepare and savour these delicacies. There she showed me how to clean the morels thoroughly and remove the millions of specks of dirt attached to them. A brush serves as the tool of choice for cleaning mushrooms, and the job was no small task, especially for an extremely meticulous food scientist. Quite a few of the mushrooms I had picked had soil at the end, which made cleaning them more difficult. Monica reminded me of what she had said about soil. As I was preparing to wash the mushrooms under running water, she pulled my hand back and scolded me. She said that no mushroom should ever be washed or it would lose its flavour. At her words my food science knowledge came back to me, and I remembered that mushroom flavours are "water soluble"—water would indeed carry them away.

We sautéed the mushrooms in hot butter and salted them just prior to sitting down to enjoy our well-earned feast. Every bite was better than the one before. It was a day and evening I will never forget. I found immense pride and a sense of accomplishment in enjoying a meal that I had had to go out and find in the wild, then take home to prepare. That evening I retold the story of my search for Kopi Luwak coffee in the Indonesian rainforests and how we ate deer meat that the tribal chief had brought to us as a gift. There is a great deal of inner satisfaction in the experience of returning to one's seemingly remote ancestral roots, hunting for bush meats and foraging for berries, nuts, and mushrooms. I suspect that people who grow their own fruits and vegetables experience a similar satisfaction, particularly in our so-called sophisticated modern society where many people's hunting and gathering experience takes place at the local supermarket. It seems that necessity and convenience have, in many cases, usurped some of our basic instincts and pleasures.

Monica had often spoken to me about her trip to Boyne City, Michigan, to attend a morel festival, the biggest of its kind in all of North America. It sounded wonderful! Since she had given me her secret hunting spot, I wanted to meet some fellow morel hunters. We decided to make the eight-hour road trip to Boyne City, Michigan, to attend the Forty-fifth Annual Morel Mushroom Hunt and Competition in mid-May.

As we neared Boyne City, signs started to appear announcing the annual morel hunt and the meeting of morel hunters from all over the northern hemisphere. Driving into the city itself, we could see that it was a beehive of activity, bursting at the seams with the influx of new visitors. Fortunately, we had planned ahead and booked at a local motel so we could at least rest from our long trip. We only had one night's stay as the motel had been fully booked for months. We only got our rooms in the first place due to a few last-minute cancellations.

After settling in, we left our motel to see the local collectors setting up their booths to sell hunt-related paraphernalia. These booths held every conceivable morel-related accessory, from hand-carved wooden walking sticks to dried morels for disappointed hunters. Some booths were dedicated to providing every imaginable sort of morel memorabilia. They were quite similar to those associated with a fan club for a sport or movie star, but instead of highlighting Hollywood or sport glamour, these booths celebrated a "dirty" and rather homely fungus! The excitement surrounding these tables was unbelievable. T-shirts with morel designs, lapel pins, earrings, necklaces, morel candles, cups, and so much more could be had, if the price was right.

Here, the usually solitary sport of morel hunting took on a different flavour and atmosphere, as hunters eagerly exchanged tales of their experiences. I heard of one hunter finding so many morels that he had to strip down to his shorts (in the middle of the woods), knot the ends of his trouser legs together, and use the trousers as a sack. If that isn't dedication, I don't know what is! I can definitely say, after further conversation with this hunter, that I had no reason to doubt his tale. I also heard ways of giving other hunters the "slip" if they inadvertently walked in while you were on the "hunt." I learned how to return the forest floor material to its original pristine, undisturbed look to ensure that no one would have the slightest inkling that the area was being monitored for signs of buried treasure—in this case, the elusive morel.

It was over these tables that we spoke of the best ways to cook morels to maximize our enjoyment of the fruits of our solitary labour in the forest. Although people presented a variety of recipes for morel cream soup, morel-stuffed chicken breasts, and morel sauces, among others, the most favoured way of preparing them was simply to sauté them with butter and sprinkle them with just a dash of salt—how simple! Evidently, collecting morels from the forest brings one back not only to the traditional way of gathering food but also to uncomplicated methods of culinary preparation involving only the bare minimum in terms of ingredients, equipment, preparation, and time. In fact, many of the highly esteemed foods we consume nowadays, such as raw oysters, sushi, and steak tartare, are prepared simply and lack the hours of culinary preparation time we tend to associate with food delicacies. Minimal preparation, however, can be a health hazard and can even cause death! You have to know with what you are dealing. Sometimes less is more in bringing out the best in foods, and sometimes even the best foods need a little help.

When the conversation turned to the subject of the largest morels ever found, it took on the flavour of tall "fish" tales featuring "the one got that away." Some even pulled out their digital cameras to show the "big one," but without a reference object—an object of known size for comparison purposes—it was difficult to determine the morel's actual size. Of course, there was a lot of laughing and pulling of each other's legs. Deer and fox hunters may have taverns in which to relay their tales, but many morel hunters have only the collector booth at the annual fair.

Surprisingly, the collector booth provided me with a unique insight into the difference between black and white morels. Privately, all the dedicated morel hunters with whom I spoke preferred black morels to white ones, though the latter are scarcer. They preferred the more intense mushroom flavours of the black morels to the milder flavours of their white counterparts. This information would become important later in my research work in the laboratory as we shall see later.

We also discussed the issue of the loss of the natural morel habitat across North America. As I've already mentioned, the elm tree was a favourite associate of the morel; morels grew well under its watchful eye. Unfortunately, the elm is scarce nowadays, as it easily succumbed to the Dutch elm disease that raced through and killed the majority of elm trees all across the North American continent. Now the ash has become the tree of choice for the morel, but just as the relationship between morel and ash was strengthening, the ash tree began to experience a similar problem with disease. It appears that morels have few friends except for the morel hunter

Monica suggested that we move quickly to secure a good camping spot in the state park for the following day. Through the mail, we had already received our permit to camp on state property during this special event. We drove off into the hills surrounding Boyne City in search of a suitable spot but many were already taken. We dared not go down the seasonal roads as it would be almost impossible to get ourselves out once we went in. Finally, we found a good spot and parked our car to get a better look. It was perfect, a well-drained location not too close to a main road.

Monica suggested that I brush up on my morel-hunting skills by taking a hike through the Michigan state forest to see if I could easily find these hidden mushroom treasures. Monica led the way out of our campsite since she knew the area better. We foraged for morels for nearly an hour with little success. We met up with some fellow morel hunters, but Monica reminded me that it was considered impolite to ask them questions about where they found their morels. Secrecy was part of the morel-hunting culture. We asked if they had arrived for the annual hunt, but they informed us that they had already been there for close to five days. Aha! So that was why we could not find any morels in the area. We moved on to look elsewhere, with no success.

When it came time to return to the car, we found that we were lost! How could we be lost when we had only walked for about an hour? But everything looked the same. I had had no trouble navigating the rainforests and remote caves of Indonesia and Malaysia, the savannahs of Ethiopia, and the semi-arid regions of Morocco. How ironic that I would choose a forest close to home in which to get lost!

As the second hour passed, and the third, we became more and more worried and frustrated. We had nothing with us except our coats—no tents, no matches, nothing at all we could use. As the fourth hour came upon us, our expressions got more and more serious, and almost fearful as the sun started to make its way below the horizon. Suddenly, I heard a rustle in the distant bushes. Could it be one of the multitudes of black bears that inhabit these parts? Where was my air horn, my pepper spray, my whistle? Monica told me to get ready to run but to hope that it was just a deer or another harmless forest inhabitant. Then, to my relief, I saw a walking stick poking out from underneath the bushes in the distance. Monica and I ran towards it. As we got closer, I called out frantically that we were lost. The hunter took out his GPS and told us to go southwest, the direction that would take us to the nearest exit which was about three kilometres away. I explained that we had been lost for hours and were afraid to go any farther. He then told us that we could simply go half a kilometre straight ahead, but that it would take us to private land, where trespassers were unwelcome and could be shot.

At that point, the chances of getting attacked by a bear or having to spend the night in the cold, wet state forest seemed much greater than the chances of getting shot. Although the probability of getting eaten by a bear was extremely remote, I had also thought that being targeted by a hungry lion in Ethiopia was also unlikely. The possibility of getting "snacked on" seemed to be a recurring theme in my travels. Perhaps the wild animals thought food scientists would be especially tasty? I hoped not! Rather, I hoped that we'd give them the trots. We asked the hunter to notify the state police that we needed help if, when he left the park, he saw a black Honda on the road with Ontario licence plates.

We made our way in the direction he had indicated. Sure enough, there was a sign indicating that this was private land and that violators would be arrested, jailed, and forced to pay a two-thousand-dollar fine. As I stepped over a broken-down fence into the forbidden property, the sight of a large hunting blind in the trees worried me. I wondered if there were people up there, ready to shoot us. Waiting for someone to call out to us, I prayed for protection. I knew in my heart that no one would intentionally do us harm, but, at the same time, we had been warned that trespassing would not be tolerated. What choice did we have, though, when we were lost and not equipped to spend the night in the forest? I hoped that anyone who stopped us would understand our predicament and let us pass through safely—preferably with some guidance as to how to find our way back.

Finally, we made it to the other side of the property and onto Chandler Hill where we had parked our car. Our relief was palpable. I had never felt happier or more exhausted than during that additional two-kilometre round-about walk to our car. That night we slept like never before. Having survived being lost in the Michigan state forest, we were ready to take on any challenge.

The following morning, the morel booths opened for business. Hundreds of morel hunters milled about, purchasing incredible amounts of paraphernalia. Some had come from as far away as Florida, California, New York, and distant parts of Canada. But whatever our origins, we all shared a passion for morels, and eagerly compared hunting techniques. When it was time for lunch, we made our way to a pavilion for a presentation by a professor of mycology (the study of fungi). She described the morel, emphasizing and re-emphasizing the importance of proper identification. Although all false morels can be a problem if consumed, the "beefsteak" morel which contains a rocket fuel component, is deadly. People have died from inhaling the cooking fumes without ever eating a bite. It would be a creative way to kill your wife, she joked, but beware—what goes around comes around!

The professor distributed examples of different types of morels and asked everyone to take a good look at them. She remarked that some people get sick if they consume the black morel with wine, which does not usually occur with the white morel. Everyone agreed, many apparently having experienced these ill effects. I wondered to myself about the reason for this particular reaction. What, if any, was the science behind this? Sometimes I feel overwhelmed by the task of separating fiction from reality. Many times, people, having heard about a supposed negative reaction to a food combination, embrace the story as fact even if it has little or no basis in reality. A communal meal of morel soup was served, reminding me strongly of a tribal hunting ritual.

From there, we moved to the tables to get our "morel licences" and register for the competition. Registration was important since getting lost in the state forest was extremely dangerous, and this was a way to keep track of the eager hunters. No GPSs are allowed on the hunt as the location of the hunt is secret.

Over 250 mushroom hunters wove through the town in a motorcade of buses. The sirens of the police escort blared like ancient horns signalling the beginning of the hunt, while people lined the streets to cheer us on. Never had I witnessed such an event or sight. All the way down the main street of the city, people would exit the shops to wave to us as we passed. I was told that this tradition went back forty-five years. I wondered where we were going and what we would find, as this part of the event, like the whole event itself, was shrouded in secrecy and little was said regarding it. This was the culmination of the events that had taken place over the last few days, and was the time when the morel would try to outwit its hunter. Soon the hushed woods would host a bevy of fevered hunters, all determined to outwit the elusive morels. In the end, with the naming of a morel-hunting champion, the morels would lose, because many would have been taken from their hiding places. Their loss would be their gain, though, because the contest would deepen the hunters' passion for the prized mushrooms.

The buses took us to an undisclosed location that had been pre-surveyed by the judges. Paramedics were on duty and an ambulance waited on standby near the buses. We were asked to remain near the buses as the rules were explained. The hunt would last ninety minutes. The ambulance siren would sound as a warning after thirty minutes and sixty minutes had elapsed, and again when only ten minutes remained in the hunt. Those not present at the judging station after ninety minutes would have ten mushrooms deducted from their total for each minute they were late.

The siren went off, and all the hunters charged into the woods like soldiers attacking enemy lines, armed not with guns but with walking sticks and compasses. They spread out over the area. Monica told me to go deep so we would not be going over what other people had already searched. For ninety minutes we worked every corner of our territory, moving between slopes, ravines, and patches of decaying wood. We collected quickly, knowing that speed was imperative. The element of time made everything so much more difficult. There was no time to enjoy nature in this fight to find the hidden morels. It was a true treasure hunt under the nerve-racking, constant ticking of the clock. Much to my surprise, I noticed that some hunters had even worn camouflage fatigues. It was amusing until I found one with a GPS device, something that was forbidden in the competition. This was supposed to be a time for us to enjoy ourselves, and to put our hunting skills and instincts to the test, not to go to extreme measures to win. It was an opportunity for some "serious" fun with a delicious outcome. I guess in every sport there will always be a few players who miss the point entirely.

When the siren went off after thirty minutes, it felt as though only one minute had passed. We would need to start moving back quickly. The next signal went off, followed by the final call. Thankfully, we made it back to the judging station on time.

Tables were set up for the judges to use to count the number of morels each hunter had collected. The numbers were recorded on a ledger and the mushrooms put back into each hunter's bag. The licences were left on the bags and the bags put on a pole to make sure they were not recounted, and to keep people from taking other people's morels and placing them in their own bags. I was disappointed with the number I had collected as the spot that Monica had given me should have yielded a lot more but, for a beginner, I hadn't done badly.

After the winner was announced, we boarded the buses but we discovered that our bus was missing one hunter. The ambulance blared its siren over and over again to call in the missing hunter. What could have happened? We were all relieved when he came running out of the woods. The whole bus roared with applause and cheers.

That evening, we roasted hot dogs over the fire and went over all the techniques we had used and looked at ways we could improve. Camping in the state forest with none of the conveniences of a regular campsite made for an interesting adventure. It was a cold evening and the fire was difficult to light. We talked for hours and went to bed, happy with the day's adventure.

Back at the laboratory, I set to work analyzing both the true white and the black morels I had collected on various expeditions into the forest. I found that morels, like many more common varieties of mushroom, have a very high moisture content. Both types of morels contained about 92 percent water. This is the reason they, like all other mushrooms, must be stored in cool places in breathable containers—paper, for example—in order to stop them from dehydrating and then spoiling. Morels were found to have a shelf life of approximately one week to ten days if properly stored. Both white and black morels had a protein content of approximately 3 percent, which agrees with the levels usually found in other common mushrooms. Though the protein contents were quite low, the amounts of essential amino acids were found to be quite good. The morels did have high levels of potassium (0.3 percent), which is important for normal heart rhythm, fluid balance, and muscle and nerve function.

Why, with such a mediocre nutritional profile, do people eat mushrooms? The answer to this question is that, although there is some nutritional benefit to the consumption of mushrooms, they are usually eaten for their flavour and the overall texture they impart to the main foods consumed in a meal. Mushrooms are usually served as a side dish or mixed in with the main foods of a meal. Since the flavour components of mushrooms are water soluble, they are easily released and incorporated into other foods, giving them the delicate flavours and essence of the mushroom. This is the reason most culinary chefs recommend that mushrooms not be washed prior to cooking. Instead, they should be thoroughly brushed clean to remove any foreign materials and small creatures. Cooking suffices to kill any undesirable micro-organisms.

Next, I conducted a series of organoleptic tests which dealt with the flavour and smell of the mushrooms. I prepared both the white and black morels, along with their white button control counterpart, by cooking them in butter and salting them just prior to serving them to a number of taste panellists. The panellists were asked to evaluate the overall flavour and texture of the mushrooms and to record their results on a score sheet. With regard to overall flavour intensity, the black morels were found to be highest followed closely by their white morel counterparts. The white button mushrooms had significantly less overall flavour intensity than their morel counterparts. There was little difference in texture between the white and black morels, but they were both significantly more solid than their white button counterparts. Although the black morels were darker in colour than the white morels prior to cooking, the difference in colour was not so dramatic once cooked, according to the panellists. Last but not least, the panellists were asked to indicate on a line graph their overall preference for the different mushrooms.

Surprisingly, though the literature asserts that white morels are slightly rarer and more desirable taste-wise than their black counterparts, the panellists expressed a slight but significant preference for the black morels. This was in keeping with the results of my informal survey of morel hunters at the morel mushroom hunt in Boyne City, Michigan. Professional morel hunters and taste panellists agree that the black morels possess a slightly more desirable flavour profile than their white counterparts. Perhaps some prefer the rarer white morel simply because of its rarity. Does rarity alone make a food desirable? The morel evidence gives this assumption the lie. Here, then, is another legend busted...or is it?

THAILAND AND MEXICO
INSECTS FOR DINNER?

My food investigations and excursions have not always been specifically scheduled or planned. I have had a number of surprises during my career. For several years I taught an International Food Law course with Michigan State University, sharing my love for travel and adventure as well as my passion for food with twenty-four American and Canadian students. We travelled to France, Belgium, Switzerland, Italy, and the Netherlands in our European Study Abroad course, and to Japan, South Korea, and Thailand in alternate years. Everywhere we went, we experienced the local culture and language, and, of course, the many everyday and exotic foods and delicacies. One of my most memorable unplanned food adventures occurred on just such a trip.

We arrived in Bangkok, Thailand, and our party of tired but eager students boarded a bus for the scenic three-and-a-half-hour ride to Suranaree University of Technology, our host university in Korat. Along the way, we remarked on the extraordinarily beautiful and largely untouched Thai countryside. Korat was a typical Thai city in every respect. We visited stores of every kind, saw people dressed in many variations of modern and traditional dress, and observed and ate at every type of street food vendor possible.

Having established our base at the university, we began scheduling our classes and other field activities. The students were particularly interested in "street foods," which are common not only in Thailand but also in many other Asian countries. What was particularly interesting about street foods was that, unlike the foods in restaurants and supermarkets, they were almost completely unregulated. Anyone could set up as a street vendor, selling food on the many street corners around the city, without being inspected in any way. The whole issue of regulations and safety became a subject for ongoing debate among this group of future food scientists. They were concerned about food safety and raised many interesting issues, one of these being the safety of the consumer. Although many food-borne illnesses have been traced back to the consumption of street foods, the number of cases is still exceedingly low, though this may be due to under-reporting.

Some of the students were intrigued by these foods, and were surprised that among the many foods sold on the street were highly priced and highly prized delicacies. Though some students were unimpressed by street foods and native delicacies, others were very vocal about the place these foods held in the local and national food culture. During one of these discussions, a Thai student brought up the interesting point that many of the street foods were not prepared at home, so banning them would mean banning part of the Thai culture and identity. She explained that many of these foods are inseparably associated either with consumption on the street or with being purchased and taken home for consumption, much like our North American "takeout" culture. Banning these street foods would be like banning ice cream cones for us, since most of us do not make ice cream at home. It would stifle a long-established cultural tradition.

When we travelled with our students, we ensured that they had every opportunity to learn, not only about the laws that govern food, but also about the local cultures. After our communal dinner each evening, which, with twenty-four students, was a feat in itself, we took the students to visit various places of cultural significance. The students were delighted to see and experience such unfamiliar objects and traditions. Cameras were always ready to take photographs and notebooks remained close at hand. For me, one particular evening stands out in my memory to this day.

On that evening, I left my students under the watchful eye of my colleague and proceeded to meet another academic colleague from the university. We drove endlessly through the narrow, darkened city streets until we reached the central core. My colleague had indicated that the night market in the city centre was an interesting place to find both modern and traditional Thai foods. As a food scientist and explorer, I could not let this opportunity pass!

At the night market, it was interesting to see the occasional car squeezing its way through the gauntlet of street vendors. The whole scene was simply awesome! No less incredible was the variety of food displayed. Roasted pork sold next to tropical fruit beverage vendors, dessert vendors, and an astonishing variety of other foods with no apparent rhyme or reason. It was a veritable food jungle, comprising every type of prepared food and food preparation equipment.

Once, I turned to see a container full of grubs crawling all over each other. The odour was indescribable and overpowering. I asked my host if this was the silkworm that had made Thailand famous worldwide as a producer of fine silk. Indeed, I was correct. But when I asked why people purchased their silkworms from a place that dealt with prepared foods, the professor told me that these were not for silk production but rather for consumption! As my jaw dropped, he commented that my mouth was positioned just right for popping such a tasty treat into my mouth. Wondering what he had been smoking, I realized he was correct when I saw a large container overflowing with the fried worms.

As I recoiled, I caught the heel of my shoe on the back end of a street vendor's cart, and turned, only to find myself standing directly in front of a heap of freshly fried grasshoppers. There must have been at least several thousand of them in each pile. The hair on my arms stood up on end. I picked up a grasshopper and, feeling the spurs on the legs, wondered if they could get caught in my throat like a chicken or fish bone. It was creepy. My Western-trained senses revolted, the tasty treats went untasted, but I did collect a few samples for later testing. Some people bring home silk; I, on the other hand, brought home the actual silkworm—fried!

Fascinated, I made my way farther into the crowd of vendors, eagerly looking for other insects, fricasseed or otherwise. The thought crossed my mind that these street vendors would never get a complaint that a bug had been found in the soup or food. I saw a variety of beetles and winged insects prepared in a similar fashion. Here in the Thai night market, I witnessed first-hand the unbounded omnivorous capacity of the human being.

I collected all the samples I could carry and returned to the hotel with my findings just like a bird returning to its nest to feed its young. In my room, I worked up the courage to taste my prey. Spider-like, I approached each fried bug cautiously. Some were spicy, while others simply defied description.

My curiosity thoroughly aroused, I investigated further. I learned that edible insects are used in traditional Chinese medicines and even as spices in certain food delicacies. The "caterpillar mushroom" (*Cordyceps sinensis*), for example, is a very rare organism that takes six years to mature. Because of their rarity, caterpillar mushrooms cost approximately ten thousand American dollars per kilogram. The *C. sinensis* begins its life cycle in the winter as a parasite on the larva of the bat moth. The summer after the fungal *Cordyceps sinensis* infestation kills the larva, a blade-like leaf develops. The leaf looks half caterpillar and half mushroom. The growth not only covers the outer portion of the fungus but also fills the dead "caterpillar's" entire body cavity; only the skin remains as the caterpillar is entirely replaced by vegetative growth. The spores are then released to invade other caterpillars. When the snow melts, the long stalks of the exposed *Cordyceps* signal the beginning of a harvest season that lasts for a mere thirty days. The *Cordyceps* must be picked quickly, before they release their spores. After the release, the compound body of the fungus wilts and eventually dries off. It was fascinating to study the evolution of a predatory parasite into a food. Not too many food scientists have looked at this one!

Cordyceps has a mild, sweet taste and releases a unique, fragrant aroma when toasted. Its usage varies throughout

Thailand, but the caterpillar mushroom is commonly reputed to improve athletic performance. The coach of the Chinese track team at the World Track and Field Championships in Germany in 1993 attributed the team's gold medals in the ten-thousand-metre, three-thousand-metre, and fifteen-hundred-metre races to this plant-caterpillar. I wondered, half amused, if it would be put on the future list of banned drugs for Olympic athletes. What would be more disgraceful—losing the medal or having to admit that you consumed caterpillar mushrooms? In any case, there was no way to know whether an athlete's winning score was solely due to consumption of a particular food or whether their win had led other people to try this very unusual food product. Even today, North American and European consumers are purchasing *Cordyceps* in caplet form from health food stores, relying on claims of body enhancement or energy-giving properties. I wonder how many know what they are actually consuming.

The use of insects as food continues to this day to be widespread. As the types of insects used are high in protein and/or fat, as well as containing many minerals and vitamins, they have long served as traditional foods and are commonly consumed in most non-European cultures. Insect consumption provides significant economic, nutritional, and ecological benefits for rural communities. South Africans feast on locusts and winged termites; in the Congo, Nigeria, and Malawi, caterpillars are popular, as are weevil larvae in Angola, honey bees in Zambia, termites in Zimbabwe, silkworms in India, crickets and locusts in Thailand, ants and fly larvae in China, grubs in Papua New Guinea, ant eggs in Mexico, Bogong moths and honey pot ants in Australia, leafcutter ants in Colombia, and stingless bees in Brazil. Grasshoppers, bees, and wasps are on the menu in Japan, whereas South Koreans enjoy grasshoppers and silkworms. Typically, these insects are used to complement other foods, either seasonally or in certain conditions such as droughts or rains.

Historically, insects were foods not only for the masses but also for royalty and the elite. In the court of Emperor Montezuma and the Aztec king who preceded him, "Mexican caviar," or *ahuahutle*, which was composed of the eggs of the aquatic *Hemiptera*, was highly prized. The eggs of several swamp fly species within this large insect family were specially prepared during a ceremony dedicated to the god Xiuhtecutli and were brought by runners from Texcoco so the emperor could have them fresh for breakfast everyday.

At the end of the three-week course in Thailand, we returned home. Not only were our suitcases and cameras full of memories but, more importantly, our minds were filled with unforgettable experiences. Upon landing in Detroit, we bid our American contingent a sad goodbye and continued our longer journey to Guelph, Ontario.

Back at my university laboratory, I carefully unpacked all the insect samples I had collected in Thailand and placed them on the bench. Various nutritional analyses yielded some very interesting results. Not only were the insects rich in protein but some were quite unexpectedly rich in unsaturated fat.

Having seen for myself in Thailand that insects could easily be incorporated into a variety of dishes, I decided to test some of them. It may seem bizarre, but as a food scientist I was aware of the growing North American trend towards spring "bug feasts," and I felt that the area needed to be investigated. Local indoor arboretums or butterfly conservatories usually host these events, and notable local or international chefs cook up all sorts of creepy-crawly delights for the public—everything from hors d'oeuvres to dessert. Surprisingly in our modern, "sanitized" society, many people eagerly gobble down the samples offered. Everything from crickets to silkworms appears on the menu, and young and old alike indulge their curiosity. What makes them do it? Is it a dare, an unsatisfied childhood curiosity about eating insects, or the prospect of trying something "forbidden" or unusual? Whatever the reason, they try them with an open mind and, more importantly, an open mouth! The television news reports stemming from these bug feasts often conclude by stating that one can purchase earthworms, crickets, and silkworms from your local pet store.

For my part, I asked a professional chef to prepare a vegetable and silkworm stir-fry, a cricket and egg omelette, and an earthworm stir-fry. As controls, I had the chef prepare the same dishes, substituting an equivalent amount of chicken for the insects. And here is one of the places where the television reports were wrong. My nutritional tests showed that dishes prepared with insects were lower in protein and higher in total fat content than their chicken-containing counterparts. Most of the total calories in the insect dishes came from fat rather than from protein and carbohydrates. Where the television reports had touted insect substitution as a way to increase a dish's nutritional value, my experimental results did not support this assertion. Here is another "made-for-TV" legend...busted!

One cannot, and must not, believe everything one sees on television. Television producers love high viewer ratings, and a program promoting the health benefits of eating insects appeals to those who enjoy watching shows such as the notorious *Fear Factor*. The truth gets lost when the focus shifts from presenting facts to convincing bug feast attendees to try these food concoctions, or to legitimizing gourmet bug dishes for the vicarious enjoyment of those who like to sit back and watch from the safety of their living rooms. When I have tried to set television news people straight on the facts, they don't care, because for them "perception is reality and reality is negotiable." Don't get me started!

Another inaccuracy in the televised insect reports was their statement that people could safely incorporate insects from local pet stores into their favourite dishes. Unfortunately, pet stores are not regulated or inspected as food establishments. Insects in pet stores have often been exposed to bacteria associated with rodents and other animals which pose a health concern. Additionally, the bedding material used for these insects—newspaper, cardboard, and other types of post-consumer materials—is not regulated for use with food for human consumption. Therefore, food prepared with insects housed under these conditions could potentially contain harmful biological and/or chemical contaminants.

My studies found that, although the incorporation of insects into Western dishes may sound exciting and even beneficial at first blush, the potential risk outweighs the questionable nutritional benefits. Insect consumption appears to be beneficial only in cultures with abundant wild insect populations uncontaminated by insecticides. As well, eating insects would most benefit people with protein deficiencies; the practice would not provide any added boost to those already eating a well-balanced diet. Just as some food for thought, I submit that some North Americans and Europeans suffer from malnutrition as acutely as the hungry people in struggling developing countries. Whereas people in developing countries lack the actual food and hence the nutrients to achieve and maintain proper health, the more privileged people in the West, however, have too much food, usually leading to nutritionally poor food choices. Break the word down and it becomes *mal*-nutrition—"bad" nutrition. The word "bad" implies two different yet related meanings; one implying inadequacy while the other being over-abundance. Still, in the end, both groups of people do not consume the nutrients they need to maintain good health. One group is suffering and dying from a simple lack of nourishing food, or the inability to afford it; a second group is also suffering and dying, but from an overindulgence in food in general, as well as from the consumption of foods that provide calories but not much else in terms of nutrition. In the first group malnutrition is involuntary and outwardly imposed, while in the second group it is self-induced.

One does not necessarily have to cross the globe to find food delicacies. While I have travelled extensively, teaching courses around the world, I have also lectured on delicacies in my own backyard. One such lecture brought me to Mexico City to discuss food delicacies with students at the Universidad de las Américas. The lecture was well received and the students were quick to inform me of the various insects that were commonly eaten in their country. In fact, a 1997 study showed that over 348 species of native insects in Mexico could be, and in many cases are, used for food purposes. While edible insects are most common in rural markets, some species command very high prices in Mexico City and other urban areas, and are purchased and sold as delicacies in restaurants.

While in Mexico, I had the unique experience of tasting a very different type of caviar. This caviar was not made of fish eggs, but rather of the eggs of a specific insect. In fact, *escamoles* are not eggs at all, but are the tiny pupae of a particular species of dark red ant. They are an extremely expensive seasonal delicacy that enjoys worldwide acclaim. Unlike my forays into remote jungles, caves, savannahs, and deserts around the world, I experienced this rare food delicacy from the comforts of a beautiful restaurant in the heart of Mexico City. Although this was a far cry from the colourful surroundings of my previous adventures, the experience of trying the food was just as exciting!

As we waited at the table to order, one of the students informed me that *escamoles* was indeed on the menu and was eager for me to try it. Why not, I thought? How about everyone else at the table? The students looked at each other and then at me, and it turned out that only one of them had ever ventured to try this exotic and expensive food. I challenged the rest of them: if I was brave enough to try this, then they would have to join me. They all agreed, probably mostly out of respect for me as a visiting lecturer. All the same, they were eager to try it together.

So, we ordered the unusual feast! The waiter informed us that the dish of ant eggs would be prepared as a cooked dip, together with ripe tomatoes and *nopales* (prickly pear cactus, minus the spines), and then properly seasoned with salt and white pepper. One of the students (the one who had tried *escamoles* before) indicated that she had been on a student exchange and had helped look for the delicacy in the arid regions of Hidalgo, north of Mexico City. After discovering the entrance to the ant nest, they started to dig very carefully so as not to lose the channel to the interior nest as it was anything but straight down. It went for approximately five metres horizontally before reaching the nest below, and all the while the ants trying to protect their nest bit them without ceasing. She told us their hands and arms were red and swollen for several hours afterwards but those who did this job habitually were not affected too much by the numerous bites as their bodies became accustomed to the contents of the bites.

When the dish finally arrived, we put it in the middle of the table for everyone to share. After having been a little put off by the student's ant tale—it was not exactly what I would have called typical table talk though it described exactly what we were about to eat—we were all still willing to try. Instead of being the first to partake of this delicacy, I indicated that the students, as my hosts, should try it first. Surprisingly, they had no problem with this arrangement, encouraging me with their enthusiasm to partake in this food adventure. I scooped some of the ant eggs along with some sauce onto a tortilla chip, and slowly and quite deliberately put the combination into my mouth. We all started laughing as I began to eat, and I almost lost my food in the hilarity! But to my surprise, it actually tasted fine. The flavour was not spicy at all, and the texture was very interesting indeed—a little like a multitude of hard-boiled eggs.

The students wanted to know what I thought. "Well," I said, "if the truth be known, I would not be fighting with any anteater or aardvark over its tasty meal, but it was not bad at all."

The conversation then returned to the student who had collected the ant eggs, and she continued with her story. She explained that timing is everything. The ant caviar must be collected at the correct moment, just before the pupae develop into actual ants. Modern manufacturing has come up with some techniques to collect the caviar, but harvesting the nests remains extremely hard and meticulous work. Legally, the nests are private property so they are well cared for and protected. The pupae are harvested from the nests three times per year, between February and late May. After harvesting, the nest is covered with grass, weeds, and *nopales*, a type of cactus, to maintain a suitable environment for the re-growth of the colony. Several kilograms of *escamoles* are harvested from each nest every season, and a nest can typically last for forty years. *Escamoleros*, the people who collect the pupae, can earn more money during the collection season than most rural people make during the entire year.

Escamoles are typically eaten by all social classes in Mexico, and are considered such a special treat that specific festivities have developed to celebrate collection times. The delicacy sells around the world for approximately eight-five American dollars per thirty-gram can. Once collected, fresh *escamoles* are extremely delicate and cannot be stored for any length of time. In contrast to the typical fish roe processing procedures, the ant pupae are not treated with high levels of salt, thus producing a milder flavour. Their low salt content makes them ideal for people with high blood pressure. Again unlike fish roe, *escamoles* are cooked, and are eaten as part of the main course rather than as a garnish or hors d'oeuvre. Although preparation methods vary, *escamoles* are usually cooked with *nopales*, an edible cactus called the "prickly pear." Legend has it that the use of *escamoles* was originally due to a native Mexican Indian's search for an alternative protein source during the spring months, before other protein-rich foods became available for collection or harvest.

Returning to Canada, I tested samples of *escamoles* purchased from different Mexican suppliers. In terms of size, the *escamole* is substantially larger than sturgeon caviar—8.5 millimetres by 3 millimetres, as compared with the sturgeon caviar's three-millimetre diameter. Moreover, *escamoles* and sturgeon caviar differ substantially in macronutrient content. Although both are high in protein per serving size as compared with other foods, *escamoles* have only 12 percent protein, as compared with sturgeon caviar at 29 percent. While *escamoles* and sturgeon caviar have approximately equal lipid contents (15 percent), *escamoles* have substantially more moisture than sturgeon caviar: 61 percent compared with 51 percent. But though the total lipid content of *escamo*les and caviar was very similar, there were dramatic differences in their fatty acid profiles. The dominant fatty acid in each is the monounsaturated C18:1, oleic acid, but *escamoles* contain 65 percent oleic acid compared with sturgeon caviar's 37 percent. Oleic acid, also found in high amounts in olive oil, is considered to be one of the "good" monounsaturated fatty acids (MUFAs) that benefit cell and heart function and has anti-inflammatory properties. MUFAs lower total blood cholesterol levels by blocking the receptors for low-density lipoprotein (LDL) production.

With these results, I concluded that the ancient collectors of *escamoles* had unknowingly found a very good and healthy food product, not only because of its high protein content but also because of its richness in heart-healthy fats. Because foods in this area were oftentimes scarce, nutritionally poor, and not very varied, *escamoles* gave the native people the opportunity to round up their diet, if only during a specific time of the year. Not surprisingly, *escamoles* were being consumed as an everyday food long before they were designated as a food delicacy.

For those who remain unenthusiastic about the idea of consuming insects, consider this: every year it is estimated that the average person unintentionally consumes just over five hundred grams of insects! One of the major entry points for insects into our food is flour which we use to make a wide assortment of foods, from bread and pasta to desserts and cereals. During the flour milling process, one of the purposes of the so-called Entolator is to smash insect parts into such small pieces that they cannot easily be seen with the naked eye. Still not convinced? Planning how to avoid products made from flour?

Moreover, the American government legally permits certain levels of non-hazardous insect parts in various foods. Chocolate, for example, can contain up to sixty insect fragments per one hundred grams, peanut butter up to thirty, and tomato sauce up to thirty fly eggs per one hundred grams. Both the Canadian and American governments permit up to twenty maggots per one hundred grams of mushrooms, approximately 320 insect parts per fifty grams of ground pepper, and less than fifty insect parts per fifty grams of flour. The list goes on and on! Ever wondered about the "cochineal extracts" on the ingredients list of certain foods and beverages? These extracts come from the cochineal insect, and give red colour to foods, beverages, and even some brands of lipstick. So let me ask: Have you ever rubbed an insect all over your lips? Have you ever kissed one? Should I continue?

INSIDE THE "CSI LABORATORY"
FOOD AND FOOD DELICACIES

Returning home from any of my many expeditions to far-off places around the world in search of the secrets behind assorted food delicacies always brings me back into familiar and "safer" territory. This is not to say that I yearn to return home, but home is where I can study these foods in much greater detail, thereby revealing things that I cannot see or measure in the field. Studying the multitude of food delicacies I bring back with me each year has turned my facilities into what some people have dubbed a special type of crime scene investigation (CSI) laboratory as many times what I find is criminal indeed! In my laboratory, I can systematically study the foods I've brought back with me and, with my fieldwork data, determine once and for all if they are truly what the world says or thinks they are, or if they belong to the category of urban myths and legends. It is by no means an easy task but, due to the advancement of modern technology and techniques, my laboratory is equipped with a number of sophisticated pieces of analytical equipment that greatly facilitate these endeavours. An episode of *CSI* could easily be filmed in my laboratory, and no one would ever guess that we were examining foods rather than blood, hair, or other samples obtained from a murder scene. The laboratory is fully equipped with all sorts of state-of-the-art gas and liquid chromatographers suitable for searching for hidden or even missing signature chemical components in foods, as well as microscopes to probe for hidden fibres—hair, for example—that contaminate many foods. Electrophoretic equipment permits me to perform protein fingerprinting and so identify my foods, just as the DNA fingerprinting often shown on television helps identify an individual. The list of equipment goes on, each piece having a specific purpose in elucidating the truths behind the foods we eat. It is very much like putting the pieces of a jigsaw puzzle together to produce one final picture.

Not only do I analyze the food I have personally collected, but I am often approached by individuals and businesses wishing to determine whether what they themselves have already purchased or intend to purchase is truly what it claims to be. Unfortunately, many of the food delicacies I have studied and am approached to examine have no officially recognized, published standards of analysis to confirm their authenticity or purity. This is where the delicacies I have collected from the field, and for which I have maintained a secure and documented chain of custody, serve as the gold standards against which I can compare the samples individuals and businesses bring to me.

Over the past few years, I have received for analysis more samples of Kopi Luwak coffee, the rarest and most expensive beverage in the world, than I would like to admit. In fact, I have received so many that I decided to publish the analytical methods I developed and utilized for authenticating this coffee in a peer-reviewed scientific journal. Although my methods were published in *Food Research International* (2004), this has not curtailed the number of sample identification requests I get, probably because I have the only reliably authenticated samples available to act as the gold standards.

The results emanating from the numerous tests I have performed have shocked me and, in some cases, disillusioned me about the honesty of some distributors and the lengths to which they will go to make incredible amounts of money. To date, of the over one hundred samples of Kopi Luwak coffee I have tested, a surprising 42 percent were found to be either complete fakes or, at best, adulterated (cut or diluted by 2 percent or more) with regular coffee beans. These statistics are shocking, to say the least! Unfortunately fraud is nearly the norm rather than the exception when dealing with a beverage for which only two to three hundred kilograms of beans are produced each year, and yet people are quite willing to wait as long as two years for this genuine coffee. The only good news behind this sad news is that the total number of frauds I have uncovered has dropped substantially in recent months. The reason for this is anyone's guess, but I suspect that a few key offenders and distributors have been adversely affected by my results and either have been put out of business or are looking for another way to deceive people.

Though Kopi Luwak coffee has been a popular subject for investigation, my laboratory has repeatedly investigated other foods as well—most notably, edible bird's nest. In 2005, I published yet another peer-reviewed article in *Food Research International*, this time examining these nests and how to ferret out the fakes. Sadly, using my newly developed methods on the various samples sent to me from around the world, problems with authenticity and purity again appeared. Of the sixty or so samples I have tested, 23 percent were determined to be either complete fakes or adulterated (cut with 2 percent or more of other products). Although 23 percent did not pass my testing criteria, there were fewer complete fakes when compared with my findings for Kopi Luwak coffee. Although the adulterated nests looked totally authentic in terms of shape, colour, and smell, they were found to be cut with materials such as karaya gum, *Tremella* fungus, seaweed, or similar ingredients. It appeared that when nests were cut with these named products—adulterants, as we call them in the field—adulteration levels seldom rose above 10 percent. I would suggest that at levels higher than 10 percent adulteration, the perpetrators were at a greater risk of being discovered, so they chose to remain at "safer" levels. Even at 10 percent, though, the additional money one would realize from such practices is enormous. With a price tag of ten thousand dollars per kilogram, an additional one thousand dollars could easily, but illegally, be obtained.

Argan oil has probably been the least adulterated of the food delicacies I have examined, but with about 16 percent of the samples tested having been found to be adulterated or complete fakes, the problem is anything but insignificant. A few "argan oil" samples I have tested have turned out to be nothing but olive oil! Although olive oil is a good oil, the dilution of much more expensive argan oil is still a deliberate act of deception used to make more money. It is a misrepresentation of a specific product, and it compromises the reputation of the genuine oil as well as that of its producers.

Testing of some pre-prepared dried morel mushroom soup bases have also produced some interesting surprises. Out of twenty mixes tested one season, two had 10 percent "half-morels" mixed in. This was serious, because half-morels should not be eaten. Two other samples had approximately 7 percent non-morel mushroom parts. On one visit to Ottawa, I found morels available for sale but discovered that they had been heavily sprayed with water, making them weigh more. Not only do we not buy water at 220 dollars per kilogram, but spraying morels with water causes them to deteriorate at an accelerated rate.

To believe that these extremely rare items are the only food delicacies subject to adulteration and product misrepresentation would be naive to say the very least. There are many more common and mainstream delicacies we all eat that are just as adulterated as these rarer foods. Over the last few years I have tested several samples of saffron, the most expensive spice in the world, which is derived from the stigma of the crocus flower, *Crocus sativus*. Saffron graces a multitude of exotic dishes served at high-end restaurants and at home. I have discovered that pre-ground saffron is susceptible to the addition of inferior parts of the saffron flower (specifically, the style), thereby diluting not only the *safranal* content responsible for the aroma, but also the *picrocrocin* content, which provides taste, and the total *crocin* content, the source of the vibrant golden yellow pigment belonging to the carotenoid family. This pigment family is also responsible for the colour of vegetables and fruits such as carrots and tomatoes. Each of these three substances impacts important characteristics (aroma, taste, and colour) for any dish containing this spice. On a few occasions, I have also found safflower floral parts added to increase overall weight.

So-called truffle oils sold in high-end delicatessens to flavour foods also frequently surface as potential problems.

The word *truffle* has its roots—pardon the pun—in the Latin word *tuber,* which means "edible root." Truffles, which are often dubbed in-ground "black (*Tuber Magnatum,* L.) and white (*Tuber Melanosporum,* L.) almonds," are a type of fungus collected in Europe with the help of either pigs or dogs. Due to their intense, highly desirable aroma, they are used to flavour various dishes from rice to pasta. Unfortunately, it has been found that the vast majority of commercially available truffle oils contain only synthetically produced truffle aroma extracts specifically Bis-(methylthio)-methane, instead of actual truffles. In a recent research trip in the fall of 2005 to San Miniato, Italy, to attend the yearly white truffle festival, I was informed by the president of the organization that this problem is rampant, and that stronger regulations are being sought and encouraged. But until then—*caveat emptor*...let the buyer beware!

So what is one to do? Not everyone has a laboratory or access to laboratory facilities. First of all, know that if the price appears too good to be true, it probably is. As with diamonds and gold, you get what you pay for. The price for the genuine article may fluctuate, but authentic items never sell for a mere fraction of the going price. Purchase only from reputable dealers that have an established clientele. Dealers that seem to have endless all-year supplies of seasonal foods or delicacies should be scrutinized to the fullest extent. Just as seasonal products such as watermelons appear much more frequently in the summer than in the winter, do not expect to find a glut of delicacies on the market when they are out of season. In addition, it may be a good idea to keep a very small amount of a particularly enjoyable food delicacy for comparison with potential new purchases.

For those who may be considering buying some Kopi Luwak coffee, which as we've seen, is highly susceptible to adulteration, purchase green coffee beans rather than roasted beans as roasted Kopi Luwak beans are adulterated more often than green beans. Green Kopi Luwak beans, according to my research work, should be slightly darker in colour than regular green coffee beans. If you see a mixture of different-coloured beans, or beans of radically different sizes, there is a good chance they have been adulterated.

Green coffee beans are more easily tested for authenticity than roasted beans, and suppliers know this. Although roasting green Kopi Luwak coffee is an added step, many kitchen-scale coffee bean roasters are very economical to purchase and simple to operate. Also, note that green Kopi Luwak coffee beans can be stored in a dry, cool place for up to two years, whereas pre-roasted Kopi Luwak coffee must be consumed almost immediately. Even in the case of regular everyday supermarket coffee (pre-roasted and/or ground), it is stale by the time it is purchased, even when sold in the most technically advanced packaging. Coffee stales within two weeks of roasting, something consumers of regular supermarket coffee have either accepted or chosen to ignore, or of which they remain ignorant.

For those interested in purchasing edible bird's nest, stay away from the nests that have been cleaned and reassembled into convenient tear-shaped discs. These types of nests, although ready to cook, are often times heavily adulterated, as the reassembly process provides the perfect opportunity to introduce other products. Instead, I recommend purchasing the slightly more expensive cup-shaped nests, in which one can still see the occasional downy feather. These nests can easily be soaked and washed in warm water, and any remaining tiny feathers can be removed with a pair of tweezers. Stay away from precooked and bottled edible bird's nest soups; more often than not, they are adulterated. Just recently (January 2006) in Hong Kong, where I did some of my work, customs officials seized seventy-five thousand bottles of processed bird's nest soup, valued at four hundred thousand American dollars, and found it to be fake.

When purchasing saffron, considered to be the world's most precious and expensive spice, remember that at two-thirds the cost of gold per gram, it is also very susceptible to adulteration. Some of the more common adulterants are ordinary spices such as turmeric and paprika. At all costs avoid purchasing powdered saffron, since not only are many of these actually composed of other hard-to-detect red-coloured spices, but if they contain saffron at all, it is the poorer quality saffron containing other non-desirable parts of the saffron flower. These fakes are even harder to detect without analytical tests. To be totally safe, purchase the actual saffron floral part, that is the red stigmas, making sure that the total number of "style" (yellow) parts is at an absolute minimum. The styles, which are the stalks connecting the red stigma to the rest of the flower, can compose up to one-third of the weight of the package, and have little or no flavour, colour, or aroma. Saffron powder is easily made at home by mixing the stigmas with a small amount of granulated table sugar and grinding the mixture with a pestle and mortar. The sugar acts as both an abrasive agent and a slight sweetener.

In the case of truffle oil, experiment with making your own by purchasing shredded white or black truffles and placing a small quantity (five grams per one hundred millilitres) in lightly flavoured olive oil and keep refrigerated between uses. Such home-prepared truffle oil may be less aromatic and flavourful than the ones purchased at the store, but you can be sure it is totally natural. The intense aromas of some truffle oils are often a dead giveaway that a synthetic extract has been added.

Consumers often ask me the reason government protection agencies are not doing more to protect them from the fraudulent activities perpetrated by these vendors selling food delicacies. Why isn't the government testing the products on the market more often and more rigorously, and why doesn't it regulate these vulnerable foods more heavily? These questions are complex, and defy simple explanations or solutions. I submit that the problem is deep, and affects everyday foods as well as delicacies. Much to everyone's surprise, although government agencies do perform random spot checks, audits, and analyses of foods, less than 1 percent of the foods we presently see on the grocery shelves have been tested by the government. This means that fewer than one in every hundred foods have gone through "compliance testing programs," which claim to provide a transparent, science-based system for assessing the accuracy of food labels and making sure foods meet current food and drug regulations. As well, given limited resources, governments appear to concentrate on more mainstream, everyday food products rather than on delicacies, since these foods are commonly considered to pose a higher health risk and greater economic loss to consumers than food delicacies. This allocation of resources often leaves the latter seemingly devoid and unmonitored.

Even more disturbing than the rarity of testing of food delicacies is the fact that, according to my work on many mainstream foods, adulteration and substitution are by no means confined to delicacies. This realization came to me as a result of my testing of many foods for various television programs on the W Network, CTV, and *Balance TV*, to name a few. In testing everything from frozen pizzas and veggie burgers to cereals, cookies, and cola beverages, my eyes were opened to a systemic problem in product ingredient compliance. There is little doubt in my mind that some food products presently sitting on people's pantry shelves are either improperly labelled or have undergone a transformation similar to that of many of the food delicacies I have studied. If you believe that all the nutritional labels that accompany food products are totally accurate, think again—my laboratory results say otherwise. I have discovered many violations of nutritional labelling standards, even with the outrageous 20 percent permissible accuracy leeway in both directions of the average (mean) value that many governments quietly give to producers. Regardless of the official displeasure engendered by my assessments as to government regulations and good manufacturing procedures (or GMP which takes into account seasonal and processing variations), as a food scientist I am obligated to voice my concerns even if only to begin a constructive dialogue or debate on the issue. Food systems in North America and Europe are safe, but we can and must do better. Let's all be thankful that governments do not permit a 20 percent leeway on car brake function, or on aircraft navigation and safety equipment! Why, though, are standards pertaining to the food we consume not more strictly enforced? Now there is a topic for debate!

TASTE DEVELOPMENT
CASE OF NATURE VERSUS NURTURE?

St. Jerome, a Christian biblical scholar from the fourth century AD, is quoted as saying that although man's sense of taste is not the noblest of his five senses, it is the one most necessary for his survival. He was correct, for it was not until the seventeenth century that food standards began to be established and the scientific understanding of food entered its infancy. Up until this time, a person's sense of taste was the only way of determining if a food was fit to be eaten or if its ingestion might lead to illness and/or death. Animals have always depended on their keen sense of taste for survival and this is the reason a rat, for example, even if starved, will refuse to eat a food that has previously made it sick.

For humans, the sense of taste both drives appetite and protects against ingestion of potentially lethal poisons. Humans from infancy like the taste of sweet foods because they have a physiological requirement for carbohydrates. The craving for salt, on the other hand, is due to the need for various electrolytes that are required in the delicate balance that controls fluid balance, muscle contraction, and the transmission of electrical signals along nerve cells. Sourness and bitterness can cause aversion and avoidance behaviours to foods, since most known poisons are bitter and some foods go sour as they spoil. Medicines that are in fact poisons if consumed at high enough concentrations are typically bitter.

Humans are considered omnivores, and need a wide variety of foods to obtain adequate and balanced nutrition for growth and maintenance of tissues as well as for important bodily functions. Together with this requirement for variety comes the natural ability of humans to adopt and consume whatever edible substances happen to become available in their immediate environment. Researchers believe that this innate adaptability implies that both cognitive learning and experience play vital roles in determining food acceptance patterns. In fact, if one looks across the globe and across cultures, one sees that dramatic differences exist in terms of not only what items are considered food but also which ones are considered valued and preferred and which ones are deemed unappealing or disgusting.

Although adult diets differ dramatically around the world, all infants begin their lives as "univores," basically consuming one universal food—milk. Some scientists even believe that human infants are innately neophobic, that is they are instinctively afraid of new foods and prefer consuming foods that are familiar to them like their mother's breast milk. It is believed that a dilemma occurs as the growing infant needs to develop and acquire a more diverse and varied diet in order to meet the nutritional needs of its rapidly growing body. How is this dilemma resolved? There are two major factors that are known to impact and shape food acceptance patterns: repeated exposure to new foods and the social context of foods during meals.

Repeated exposure to new foods begins very early in life. In fact, it starts when the infant is still consuming breast milk as its sole food source. The child's taste preferences begin to develop during breastfeeding as flavours from the mother's diet appear in the breast milk itself. Scientists have found that children can learn not only to accept but also to enjoy new foods after repeated exposure to them, and that children's initial rejection of a new food is actually quite normal.

The social context at mealtimes is also very important, as routine family meals teach children about their rules of cuisine—which foods their culture deems edible and which it does not. The child not only learns which foods to eat but also, implicitly, which foods not to eat: those excluded from the diet. As well, the child learns what is perceived as disgusting and taboo to eat. Food combinations are learned in relation to certain cultural norms, for example that ice cream can be added to fruit but not to meat. Parents' beliefs also play an enormous role in food acceptance, for example the notion that pork or beef is not acceptable for consumption on religious grounds.

It is in this context that even those foods which are considered delicacies inspire horror or disgust on tables around the world.

It should be remembered that food is one of the few things that becomes intimately associated with our bodies through our contact with it. Since it is physically internalized, it becomes, in a sense, a part of us. As the saying goes, "You are what you eat," and the foods we eat become something by which we identify ourselves. Food fulfills this role so well that many religious traditions around the world use food in their sacraments in order to deepen their spiritual force.

In North America, rats are considered to be filthy and disease-carrying vermin since they consume garbage and live in sewers. To consume such a "food" would be to allow these undesirable features to become intimately associated with oneself. But in parts of China, the grey rat, which lives in forests and fields and doesn't eat garbage, is considered a wholesome and respectable food.

In the same way, consumption of delicacies is a means of identifying oneself with the world of leisure and wealth. It has been said that 60 percent of people who eat at high-end gourmet restaurants worldwide are not rich but rather of the middle or lower economic classes. They are not there to satisfy their hunger but to experience a gustatory delight. This has been true ever since the eleventh century, when the first restaurants were established in China.

It is interesting to note that, although people around the world are basically identical in terms of their physiology, not everyone perceives any given food as being equally good-tasting or of value. In dealing with the obvious and important question "What is good taste?" scientists primarily look at social, religious, cultural and historical influences. Some have noted that the nobility in Europe were driven by a strong desire to set themselves apart from the lower classes through gluttony and extravagance in their everyday diet. This became a key driving force behind the advancement of European cuisine. From the late Middle Ages around the eleventh century, there was a marked increase in trade and travel, and the food supply improved significantly for the lower classes, prompting the nobility to use luxury goods such as precious spices—saffron, cinnamon, nutmeg, and pepper—to set themselves apart from the lower classes.

Human beings enjoy to indulge in foods that go far beyond the need for simple nutrition; and it is this curiosity that drives us to consume delicacies that no longer simply supply calories and nutrients, as do everyday foods, but brings the consumer to a place where he or she can partake in a history, a culture, and a story (something that is not usual with most other foods). People in general have become progressively more distant from the source of their everyday foods, and have therefore lost the important stories of these foods' origins and compositions. Delicacies in many cases are simply variations of typical foods we know and love, such as coffee, cheese, oil, and mushrooms, but with food delicacies the history and associations are intact, rich, and interesting. The whole concept of a food delicacy is often related to how rare it is, or how difficult to obtain. This usually translates into foods of extremely high price. For you to drink a cup of Kopi Luwak, someone had to search the dangerous jungles of far-off lands. For you to enjoy bird's nest soup, someone must have risked life and limb (not to mention contact with gangsters) to get at the swiftlet nests in remote caves in the Pacific. It is in obtaining and consuming these hard-to-get foods that one gains the right to brag that one has eaten something rare and highly esteemed.

Scientific tests performed in my laboratory, although they showed some differences between the delicacies and their more common counterparts, generally indicated that there was not a huge difference between food delicacies and those foods that are easier to obtain, cheaper, and more commonly consumed and accepted. Where the differences in processing may lead some to question the safety of the delicacy as compared with its more common counterpart, science has shown that the delicacies are indeed safe to consume. Science was also able not only to come up with rapid methods to determine the adulteration of these foods but also to show that food delicacies, like other products on the market, are subject to imitation for the monetary gain of a few.

It is interesting to note that science can tell us the composition and therefore the cost of everything we eat, but can tell us the value of nothing. The value placed on any food is subjective, determined by the individual or society; food science can only serve to protect an individual's right to safe, wholesome, and unadulterated foods. Basically, food delicacies remain, and will remain for the foreseeable future, solely a matter of taste, and this should serve as "food for thought" for all of us.

"If I were you, I'd sooner eat this book than eat the food described in it. But definitely read it first. It's fascinating."
—Steve Hartman, CBS Correspondent, *60 Minutes* and
CBS Sunday Morning

Talk about food for thought!... If you have ever wondered exactly what you're consuming in that piece of cheese or cup of coffee, you will be shocked and amazed by the revelations here. And if you are at all squeamish, this book will help you lose a few pounds!
—Anna Wallner, Co-host, *The Shopping Bags: Tips Tricks, and Inside Information to Make you a Savvy Shopper*

Dr. Marcone's search grants us the privilege of journeying to places in foreign lands that would rarely be visited by the average traveler. Danger, mystery, and the magical unveiling of urban food myths grip the reader with a strong pull of curiousity and wonder. A unique and surprising experience. This book is educational, rewarding, and a joy to read.
—Beverley Elliott, Actress and Singer